BEST NEBRASKA TEEN WRITING

2024

VOLUME 2

BEST NEBRASKA TEEN WRITING

2024

VOLUME 2

Hastings College Press | Hastings, Nebraska

Copy edited and typeset by Ava Brackhan.

ISBN: 978-1-942885-93-1

Contents

critical essay

personal essay & memoir

senior portfolio

Introduction

As an Affiliate Partner of the Alliance for Young Artists & Writers, Hastings College is honored to celebrate the winners of the 2024 Nebraska Scholastic Writing Awards. We invited students age 13 and above from all 93 counties within the state of Nebraska to submit their writing in one of ten categories, such as Critical Essay, Poetry, and Short Story. Graduating seniors also had the option of submitting a Writing Portfolio, a collection of works that demonstrate the writer's technical versatility. All of this year's 155 submissions were read and scored by a jury of Hastings College faculty, staff, and students. The original work featured in this publication showcases the creativity of our Honorable Mention award recipients.

The Scholastic Art & Writing Awards program, established in 1923 by Maurice R. Robinson, the founder of Scholastic Inc., identifies teenagers with exceptional artistic and literary talent and brings their remarkable work to a national audience. All works are blindly adjudicated based on originality, technical skill, and the emergence of personal vision or voice, first on a regional level by more than 100 local affiliates of the Alliance, and then nationally by an impressive panel of industry experts. Students at the regional level are awarded an Honorable Mention, Silver Key, or Gold Key distinction. Gold Key work then advances to national adjudication to receive Gold Medals or Silver Medals. Each region also nominates works for American Voices & Visions Medals, the highest regional honor.

Annually, the Alliance partners with individuals, foundations, and corporations to offer scholarship opportunities for students in certain categories or addressing particular themes. National Medalists' works are published in national publications and on the Alliance's website, artandwriting.org. Select writing is published in *The Best Teen Writing* annual anthology. The Alliance strives to teach young students to develop a strong creative capacity along with celebrating the role of art and literature in society.

Dr. Cat Clifford
Hastings College
Hastings, NE

SCIENCE FICTION & FANTASY

THE FIGURE

KENNA PFEIFER

Grade 9. Adams Central Junior Senior High School, Hastings, NE.

Walking alone down a long winding path, Mary could make out what appeared to be a large hooded figure standing at the top of the hill. It was almost the middle of the night, and there was barely any light coming from the moon since it was supposed to start storming in an hour. She didn't quite know what the thing on the hill was and brushed it off as a trick of the light, but as Mary approached that part of the path the figure stood on, she knew it was not a trick of the light. As she got closer to the strange being, it startled and darted down the path. Not knowing who or what this was, Mary thought it best to chase after it and make sure it wasn't leading her to somebody who needed her help.

As she sprinted, she realized that this might not be a smart idea. *What if this person was one of her adversaries or some blood thirsty person?* However, Mary didn't think anything of it and continued to chase after the creature. The figure was surprisingly quick and didn't show any sign of slowing down. Mary was struggling to keep up. They came to a fork in the road, and the figure turned to the left, leading Mary down a path that was getting increasingly dark. After what seemed like a lifetime of running, she saw the creature stop and grin, then disappear.

Mary hurried over to the spot where the figure had disappeared. She spun in circles trying to find out where the creature had gone. It was only then that she realized she didn't know where she was. Out of the corner of her eye, she spotted a shadow dash across the path. She slowly made her way towards the shadow, careful not to startle it. Mary reached the shadow, but when she looked around, she noticed that she was in the middle of nowhere in the middle of the night. She noticed that there was a strange amount of light coming from between the trees. Mary was very conflicted whether or not to go and check it out. After a few minutes of weighing the pros and cons, she decided to go peek through the trees and make sure it was safe to go through. Mary concluded the area was safe—no one was going to pop out and bludgeon her to death.

The minute she came into the clearing she saw what looked to be a lift of some sort. Mary walked over to it and got in just to see what was there. The door slammed closed and locked behind her—the only handle was on the outside of the door. Mary whipped around just in time to see the figure from earlier that had disappeared. Mary was confused and exasperated. She tried to bust down the door, but the situation was irresolvable. The figure disappeared again, but this time Mary heard a snap behind her. She turned around and sure enough, there was the figure standing right behind her. It had no face. Its robes were black and very torn. Mary started to panic. She was praying that this creature was there to help her, not hurt her. The creature seemed to have read her mind, shaking its head. With one swift motion, the creature created a dark mass that consumed Mary and the lift. The creature snapped its fingers and any evidence of what had just happened was gone. This figure returned to the spot in the road where Mary had first spotted it and waited for its next victim to walk down the path.

FLASH FICTION

A Grand Adventure

Rebekah Daily

Grade 11.

When he was smaller (smaller than four, that is), all the Boy knew to do with the Cat was to rub its ears, hold its tail, and pet its long, wriggly back—like most people. But sometimes, when one is very special, a boy turns four and a part of them knows to Follow the Cat. This knowledge cannot be learned, and it cannot be studied. It can only be found. Undoubtedly, the wisdom to Follow the Cat is rare. But for those in whom it takes root, there is nothing less than a Grand Adventure awaiting them.

The Boy was one such serendipitous child. When he turned four, though he did not recognize it and probably never could have explained it, a part of him awakened to the knowledge of how and why to Follow the Cat. It didn't take him long to pursue this newfound intuition, for the family barn Cat was often snaking by his legs and nudging him with her head. She recognized, of course, a boy who knew. Once, to test him, she slunk away from the Boy, pausing briefly to check if he was Following.

Of course he was Following. He knew.

The Cat padded past the house where the Boy's parents sat conversing on the porch. The Boy padded too. The Cat whispered by the old woodshed. The Boy whispered too. Then, the Cat slipped between the rows of corn growing up some hundred yards from the old farmhouse. The Boy slipped through right behind. He knew that—though his parents had often warned him never to play in the corn—Following the Cat could lead to no harm. He didn't know how he knew, but it was knowledge nonetheless.

The Cat leapt lightly over dry, fallen cornstalks and avoided the sharp edges of the green, but drying husks. As she went, she silently taught the Boy to do so as well. Once, she forgot to teach the Boy how to avoid a puddle that she had neatly leapt over, and the Boy plodded right through it, getting mud down his socks, between his toes, and all the way up to his knees. Still, the Boy Followed the Cat. Once, she ducked through a small gap between cornstalks, barely large enough for herself. Still, the Boy Followed the Cat, though it was much harder for him to get through. Once, she got distracted by a caterpillar and dove after it, trying to catch it for a snack. Still, the Boy Followed the Cat.

Finally, the Cat came to rest in a tiny lea between two cornfields. The Boy had no idea where he was, but he knew that when Following the Cat it was impossible to be lost. Not knowing where one's self is and being lost are not the same thing, he knew. He didn't know how he knew, but it was knowledge nonetheless.

The Cat paused to lick her delicate paws, looking like a shapely vase standing still in the middle of the field. Because he was Following the Cat, the Boy stopped too. The Cat lay down in the damp dirt; the Boy lay down too.

Something appeared in the corner of the Boy's vision. Not quite a sparkle, not quite a reflection. It looked like a liquid capsule of light. The Boy tentatively reached out and touched it. The Thing was hard and smooth and round in his small hand. It didn't shy away when he touched it. It was Friendly. The Boy slipped the Friendly Thing into his pocket.

The Cat stood up again, so the Boy stood up. She seemed pleased with herself. She knew that the Boy had found what only she could show him. The Cat started home. The Boy followed much better this time, as he had much more practice. When the Cat leapt lightly up onto the porch of the farmhouse, the Boy Followed. She stopped. He stopped.

"Where have you been?" the Boy's mother asked. She did not notice the Cat, or the way the Boy protected his pocket where the Friendly Thing lay. She only noticed that the Boy was filthy.

"I have had a Grand Adventure," the Boy explained gravely. "For I have Followed the Cat, and she led me to this."

Proudly, the Boy reached into his pocket to show his mother the Friendly Thing he had found, as evidence of where he had been and what he had done.

"That's a pretty marble," his mother said.

The Boy shook his head. It was not a marble, he knew. How sad that his mother did not! No, no the Friendly Thing was powerful and undeniable proof that he had Followed the Cat. The Boy didn't know how he knew, but it was knowledge nonetheless.

Skirts and Dresses

Cassandra Wong

Grade 12. Millard South High School, Omaha, NE.

"Is there anyone you'd like me to call, Miss?"

"No." She paused. "No, I'm alright."

The nurse handed her a few cards, before handing her a fresh set of hospital-branded sweats.

The woman went home and chucked the shredded skirt into the bin. Its presence seemed to offend her, the cheap pleather laughing at her. The stain of the Bachelorette shot from the night before smelled faintly of vodka. She wobbled on shaky legs to her shared bathroom, and stifled a sob at the sight of the matching "mister" and "missus" towels hanging innocently above the counter. She twisted the knob of the shower to scalding hot, letting the steam coat her skin. The water burnt her feet, then her knees, turning her body a blotchy pink. Scrubbing at herself, she sunk to the base of her shower, tucking her knees into her breasts, and cried.

Hours later, he came home. He found her wrapped in her old college sweats, curled up in bed. He stared at her back, watching it rise and fall as she slumbered. A smile stretched across his face. He was so lucky to be able to call this woman his.

She stiffened as he slid into the bed beside her.

"Hey, beautiful."

"Hey."

Their voices were soft in the late morning sun, and she shifted, rolling to face him.

"Did you have fun?" he asked, tucking a lock of dull blonde behind her ear.

"Did you have fun?" the man panted, pinning her wrists against the brick.

"Yeah," she lied. "I had fun."

"Stop it, I can't, I don't."

His eyebrows furrowed, scanning her face. He opened his mouth, but closed it when her gaze flitted down.

"That's good," he said. "Get some sleep."

The girls were ecstatic. It was the final fitting session for her dress. They chittered around, giggling and snorting as they waited for her to enter and show them all one last look at the bride-to-be. The knob jostled, and in she came, tripping over the long train. The girls cooed, fussing over the lace arms and the beaded bodice. She took a doe-like step forward, and oh, shit, the heel caught on the train, and a rip pulled its way up the skirt. Her breath hitched.

He had ripped her best "I'm young and sexy and you can't have me" skirt.

"Oh, baby, don't cry. The tailor can fix it!"

"Do you like that, baby?"

"You can fix it, can't you?"

Her pleather skirt she'd scandalously bought among friends was in tatters. He'd got her.

"Whatever do you mean? It's so very clearly an accident. Who makes things that delicate these days?" The maid of honor fussed. "Whatever happened to quality!"

"Such a delicate thing." His breath smelled of fish and stale beer. "You bruise so easily." He slid his thumb along the seam of her underwear.

She turned, running her way through the dressing room, further ripping the dress. The sobs gurgled at the base of her throat. Her chest caved in, and she hiccuped as her face grew wet.

"Please let me go," she'd said.

"Hey," he said.

"Hi," she said, back turned towards him.

"I heard from Amy about the dress, and baby—"

"You like that, baby?"

She closed her eyes.

"We need to talk," she said, because skirts and dresses aren't the same.

SHORT STORY

Through These Bones

Marcus Luevano

Grade 10. Northwest High School, Grand Island, NE.
Natalie Starostka, Educator.

As I walked to school, the sun on my back projected my thin shadow in front of me, reminding me of my nickname, "Bones"; however, it was imperative that I walk to school with temerity so I didn't lose my reputation on the first day. When I arrived at school, I navigated my way through the hallways filled with the perverse words of all of the other students. Then there was Elias standing in the corner. The placidity in his face told me that he had yet to find a good reason to fight anybody. Most days he didn't need a reason. Elias and I were total opposites in appearance but identical in upbringing. We were both beleaguered by families that didn't care about us at all. The irrefutable truth was that we didn't need them because we had everything we needed in each other. I had the smarts that Elias wanted, and Elias had the strength that I needed. We'd always been friends with each other. Nothing ever changed for us. I always followed Elias everywhere he went. Then before I could even say a word Elias said, "Hey, Bones, want to get out of here?"

I responded simply by saying, "Sure." We then made our way out of the school.

We found ourselves outside of the Grand Island theater, which closed this past year (1952).

Upon first glance, we saw that the basement window was open. There were no security alarms or police to deter the two of us from entering the theater, so we crawled through the window and sat down on some worn out theater seats.

After a brief period of silence, Elias asked, "So, what trouble have you been getting into lately?"

I wanted to tell Elias that I hadn't done anything troublesome, but I lied instead and said, "I almost got caught stealing a candy bar from the gas station the other day, but I ditched it before the clerk could get me. How about you, Elias? Don't you have court coming up?"

"Yeah, but court isn't a big enough deterrent to keep me from fighting and breaking into places. Sounds like if the judge sees me again, I'll be put away for a while. What should I care? I have nothing better to do."

I could see where this conversation was going, so I tried to extract myself from it by walking around the theater, which used to shine with iridescent lights. It was crazy to think that just two years ago everyone in town was rushing through these doors to see the latest movie. Now it was only Elias and me filling the theater with words.

After our reprieve from the outside world, Elias and I left the theater and began our journey home via the alleys. As we were walking that night, we could hear the atrocious sound of mice running rampant through the trash cans and gutters. The shouts of arguing families and friends reached us sporadically as the two of us walked on. In the distance, we saw a shadow. Instantly I knew who it was. It was none other than the illustrious trouble maker, Randle. He was the whole reason Elias was walking on thin ice. When Elias and I finally met Randle face to face, there was a dismal silence between the two of them.

Then Randle asked, "Hey, Elias, isn't it funny meeting you here?"

Elias responded strongly by saying, "Yeah, I see that scar on your face. I've got to admit it looks good on you. For some reason it looks familiar."

"How do you like walking on the tightrope, Elias? Bones! You better tell your family to quit rationing their food. A twig like you won't survive when Elias gets put away."

"Randle, you better shut your mouth before a scar is the least of your worries," Elias lashed back.

"Come on, Elias. Either we fight or you lose your reputation, and I'd hate for that to happen," Randle said deviously.

I knew Elias could not do this alone, so I tried my best to emulate his tough look by feigning a grim face. Inside, I was filled with trepidation concerning what was about to go down. Elias' abhorrence for Randle was so thick that it could be cut with a knife. I knew I had to do something; however, there was nothing around to fight with. The only thing I had were my words.

When I saw Elias clenching his fist fervently, I yelled, "You're better than this! Just walk away for once!"

"But I can't. I can't lose this fight," Elias rumbled.

"Yes, you can, Elias. You're better than this!"

Once Elias heard my words again, he instantly backed off and we began to walk away.

Randle responded in a slick tone. "Elias, you're really going to walk away from a fight because of what your skinny friend said?"

When Elias looked back, I told him, "Just keep walking." That's when I turned around, mustered all of the strength I'd gotten from Elias over the years, and punched Randle square in the jaw. Randle tumbled to the ground and felt the filth of the back alley. My rage-filled fist continued to punch Randle's bleeding face as I hovered over him. I was no longer thinking. I could no longer control my fists. The blows came faster and faster as the adrenaline coursed through my veins. Randle's once golden hair was now matted with the filthy mud from the alley. When Elias realized that any attempt to intervene would be futile, he listened to my words and just kept walking. Shortly after, I was pulled off of Randle and placed in a cop car by two police men. Once I was done with him, he was reduced to nothing but pulp. I could see the two police men asking Randle what I'd done to him. When the cops returned to the car, they opened the door and said, “Just walk away, son.” When I got out of the car, I could see my freed friend walking. I knew I was my own person now and went the other direction.

Snowy Owl

Jihye Seo

Grade 10. East High School, Lincoln, NE.

The Snowy Owl ruffled her feathers as she bathed in the attention that was suddenly cast upon her. Dozens of cameras lined up towards her and humans looked up now and then to admire her. It felt great, except for the awful heat that stuck on her feathers. She tapped on the roof of this "house" structure, feeling uncertain about whether she had chosen a good place for enough attraction.

This whole mission had been discussed with her family beforehand, a project called, "Warning." The whole avian community had been flying about in an attempt to inform the pesky, ignorant humans about the maddening chaos that they are causing in the avian nest.

Snowy Owls were a top pick to inform these humans, great at attracting attention in warm places that weren't fit for them. Her kind spanned from Colorado to Pennsylvania over the course of the last 10 years, shocking many birders and popping up all over the news. But that didn't last too long.

Humans somehow managed to forget about them and their work, their countless sweat-filled days of protesting under the sun without a glimmer of snow. Year after year, time after time, they grew more hopeless. She was her kind's last chance. With her head held high, she surveyed the spectators below. According to her dad, this audience was a bigger audience compared to his 6 years ago.

Her dad had been on the Colorado mission, shocking experts as they quickly found out it was a hungry youngster looking for food, escaping from the growing competition in the north. But boy were they wrong. He believed in humans. He knew they would be able to change their ways of living. He sought to compromise with them. But his visit left no lasting effect as his existence was forgotten.

A few years later, it was her turn to step up. She had chosen Southern California for her destination, determined to leave a lasting effect on these forgetful humans. The journey was long and perilous, too difficult for her to remember anything. She would rather put it in the past. At the moment, the conditions were perfect. It was crisply hot and the audience was getting excited by every passing second, their minds buzzing with questions.

In fact, she managed to see someone cautiously taking away her pellet in a very stealthy way. The person was eager about it but she laughed at this. She doubted anything would come from that. After all, her diet stayed the same with the same rodents and small animals she could get her talons on.

Suddenly, a murderous cawing fished her out of her train of thought. Above her orbited a group of crows, clearly disturbed by her presence.

"What are you doing here?!" they shouted defensively, their wingbeats getting harsher by the minute.

"It's for the Warning," she informed, keeping her voice down. Snowy Owls must always maintain their gracefulness.

"Well, that thing has been failing for a mountainous time, eh?" a crow mocked, landing right next to her. His shiny black feathers reflected the glaring sun, slightly blinding her.

"This is our last try. We won't do anything after this one. One final chance," she explained as her beak clicked in frustration.

"Well, you lot give them one too many final chances, that's for sure," the crow commented, cawing out a laugh at the last word.

The Snowy Owl rolled her eyes in annoyance, chirping a threat to the crow. The crows responded to this in fright, flying away when she attacked and coming back when she was stopping to rest. "Unfazed,

unfazed, act unfazed," her mind chanted every time she raised her wings to chase the crows away.

But she couldn't simply act unfazed. Luckily, crows weren't a new cause of her anger. They were always after her in some way whenever she wanted to venture south. She had her way of dealing with them. But, unluckily, this was during her mission. Therefore, with nervousness stuck on her head like mice bones on owl pellets, she couldn't keep calm.

Finally, she flapped her giant wings as a threat and flew towards the orbiting crows. The crows grimaced and cawed shrilly at this, frowning before flying away into the sky. It was always the less predatory birds that decided to be irritating. An eagle or a hawk would never act like that. But she certainly had more important things to think about.

Were Snowy Owls the ones that were doing things wrong here? Were they not supposed to act this way? Was she not the last chance? Was she a fake last chance? Questions took flight in her brain for a sliver of an hour, consuming her with dread. What if these humans won't change? What if they persisted on to live the way they have always lived?

Her brother on his Fort Worth mission proudly said that he was sure he made a great influence. The people were amazed to see him, wondering how far he flew to get that far. Curious about how he managed to survive his flight. Questioning where he will go from then on. But soon, they forgot about him.

She shook her head in denial and ruffled her wings once more. This was just nervous thinking, not her. Surely the heat had a serious side effect. She trotted down to the base of the roof, inspecting the area as the sun began to set on the horizon. Her feathers fluttered at the slightest warm winds of Southern California and she breathed in what she could of the salty smell of the warm sea. The heat, the trees, and the people were all an addition to her tiredness but interesting things. She rarely felt or saw these back in the cold tundras or open fields in the winter. So, she took in everything she could from the city lights to the oddly paved pavements.

Eventually, she yawned. This place was exhausting and the heat was clipping off her stamina by every ticking hour. She needed a rest and she certainly needed to get out of here. So that's exactly what she did. She took off, her wings beating harder than any other Snowy Owl, heading for home.

NOVEL WRITING

Keep It Under Cover

Erinn Briggs

Grade 10. Lakeview Junior Senior High School, Columbus, NE.

After I've changed into my silk nightwear and taken my contacts out, I settle into my comfortable bed. When I lean against the ornately carved headboard and sip my cucumber mint hot tea, the steam fogging up my glasses, I can't help but wonder where my mom could potentially be. Maybe she's in the private jet, being tended to by the resident doctor, Dr. Princeton. The plane could be flying over Greece or Italy, the clouds so thin that all the stars can be seen out of the bulletproof windows.

I blow out a breath, and for the first time, I feel a sense of loneliness. Even though my brother is here, he's busy with his friends. Yes, I do have Veron, but he has his own job. He's *supposed* to be here for my every need.

All of a sudden, I become a little kid again. I'm not a spy anymore. I'm someone's daughter, wondering if her mom will actually survive this mission. No matter how many times she comes back home, I end up worrying if she'll survive the next one.

I can't control it. It just happens.

When I finish off my tea, I set it on the wooden nightstand, taking off my glasses as well. I pull the layers of blankets and quilts over my shoulder and ear, snuggling my head into the fluffed silk-covered pillows. As soon as I'm all settled, I let out a breath. Warmth fills my limbs and I smile a little bit as the lights dim. With the fire crackling and the rush of wind pounding against the window, a comforting feeling forms in the room. School feels like my second home, but it doesn't have the same feeling as this room, even if my friends are there.

I feel my eyes drift closed, my muscles relaxing and almost melting into the mattress. Soon enough, the sound of the wind and the crackling of the fire melts into the darkness behind my eyelids, and everything goes quiet.

"Hey, kiddo."

A gentle, cold hand rubs my shoulder, and my eyes groggily blink open, finding the green eyes of my mother gazing down at me, her lips pulling up in a soft smile.

Immediately, all sense of tiredness goes away. "Mom!" I exclaim, wrapping my arms around her, my mother laughing and returning the gesture. We stay like this for a solid three minutes and forty-three seconds until I pull away.

Catherine Abernathy is already wearing her formal attire: a deep purple pantsuit, her hair in a sleek bun tied back with a matching purple ribbon. From the looks of it, she's already been up writing reports on her mission and sending them to NATO headquarters.

"I have raspberry pancakes and apple juice waiting downstairs. We'll catch up there, alright?"

I nod, pulling back the covers and snuggling my feet back into my slippers before following her out of my room.

As we pass the wing where my brother and his friends are staying (each of them gets their own room), Mom gives me a concerned look. "Sorry you were on your own yesterday, Illa. I didn't expect to be gone that long."

I shrug a shoulder, already past it. "You're here now," I say, and Mom smiles.

I pull a stool from the lounge counter and climb onto it, the smell of hot pancake batter and raspberry extract drifting to my nose. Mom holds up two plates of steaming pancakes and sets one in front of me, putting the other one in her spot next to mine. Then, she gives me a fork.

Before I can dig into the delicacy, Hadley Gorindale, my mom's personal assistant, comes in with a wad of mail in her hand. "The deliverer came," she says, something strange in her eyes. "There's something you need to see."

My mom frowns, giving Hadley a nod before accepting and going through the letters. One must catch her eye because her body freezes.

She sets the letters on the table, the others immediately forgotten about as she grabs her letter opener and tears at the already luxury-looking envelope. Two pieces of paper are hidden inside, what looks like a formal invitation and a quickly scrawled half piece of paper.

Mom's eyes scan across the paper, going at least seventy miles per hour, maybe more. Her hands start to shake a little and she bites the inside of her cheek. Once she stops, she looks at me, annoyance and intimidation mixing in her eyes at the same time. "This isn't for me."

She hands me the letters, letting out a deep sigh. "What? Another mission?" I ask, glancing down at the invitation.

"Read the report first." Her voice is firm, and I nod vaguely.

"Okay, then."

My mom disappears down her office hallway, and a few seconds after that I hear the sound of her voice, then another, static one responding. She's making a call.

I look back down at the letter and the report, narrowing my eyes.

> To Agent Monarch,
>
> This is an invitation to the Monaco Royal Convention, where the esteemed Grimaldi jewels are going to be showcased. Across Europe, there have been reports of a shady girl and an older man, always researching things and going to museums. Especially the British Museum. They have been spotted there more than once, looking at the necklace of Catherine of Aragon and some other priceless artifacts of the matter.

They have forged invitations to the Monaco Royal Convention. Our trackers say they have bought plane tickets to France with fake IDs. Not only are they wanted under different names, but they are connected to Prism Corporations. You already know who they are.

You need to track them, Monarch. They are going to steal the Jewels of Grimaldi. And they are going to run, then sell them on the market for a high, high price.

Agents Parrotfish and Independence will be with you. As soon as this letter arrives, you will be getting more information on when and where.

I've been doing all I can to make this an easy journey, but Empire is getting worked up. You are a very talented agent, Monarch, and you must stay focused. Any distraction will harm the mission, and it will cause the jewels to be lost forever. You know that once they go up on the Market, they will never be seen again. At least, not in our territories.

We have complete faith in you.

—Mockingbird

My mom's voice is yelling now, but I'm too shocked to listen. Prism Corporations are back? WorldTech wants me to track them down? The Grimaldi jewels are going to be stolen?

With a sigh, my mom walks back into the room, her cheeks flushed and her arms crossed. "I can't go with you, honey. I tried to cancel on the Prime Minister, but WorldTech and I both know it's too important. You're on your own."

I frown. "Isn't that against code, though?"

She nods. "You're still going with someone, but it's not going to be me. I'm sorry, I wish I could guide you through this, but your cover—"

"Might be blown, I know." I sigh, running a hand through my hair. "I'll be fine."

Mom hugs me, and I just sit there. Do I have to be gone? Already? And I'll miss Thanksgiving, the best holiday of the year. I'd be okay with Easter or the Fourth of July, but not the official start of the holiday season.

Not only that, but I can't have my phone. My texts and calls would be too easily tracked, so I can't communicate with my mom or my friends.

With a begrudging sigh, I put the report on the table and examine the invitation. Maybe this will all be over within a few days.

"Illiana," my mom calls up the stairs. "Are you ready? The jet will be leaving soon."

I sigh, slinging my backpack over my shoulder when it seems I am just putting it down. I glance at my room once more, the bed made perfectly just as it was when I returned only two days ago, my hutch cleared off and closed.

"Yeah, coming," I reply, pushing my door open and shutting it gently behind me once I've stepped through.

My colleagues are already on the plane when I get to the tarmac. Eleanor Crawford is someone my brother has worked with before, a proper English spy trained in the undercover version of Cambridge. And, well, of course, there's Howard Hamilton, a grumpy college-aged mercenary working for the President of the United States. He's been given only a couple of honorary awards, including just a casual Presidential Medal. Nothing too drastic.

"Illiana." Eleanor nods, giving me a polite smile. "Nice to see you again."

I nod back, glancing at the irritated Howard. "What?" he hisses dryly, and I shake my head.

"Sorry," I mutter, turning back to my mom.

She gives me a sideways half-smile, raising her eyebrows in an "I'm sorry" kind of way. "My little junior is all grown up," she says, tilting her head and coming up the plane stairs to give me a hug.

"I'll be back, Mom," I say into her shoulder, seeing a glimmer in her eyes that's usually not there. "I'll be fine. I promise."

She just nods, giving me one more squeeze before stepping back down the stairs. "I love you!" she calls as the stairs fold in. "And good luck!"

The door seals before I can respond, and Eleanor puts a hand on my shoulder. "It'll all work out, Illiana. I promise. I was you when I was younger, and my mom still does that. You're going to do great."

I nod, forcing a smile to come to my face despite all the worries that are flurrying inside of my heart. From now on, tomorrow isn't promised.

"Here," Howard grunts as he digs through the plane's surprisingly large closet, tossing an elegant dress to Eleanor. "Wear this. We're coming up on Monaco."

I roll my eyes as she hands the blue floor-length dress to me, an apologetic look on her face. "You'll get used to it," she says. "I had to. He's just ... experienced."

"More experienced than *you,*" Howard says without looking at her. "And way more experienced than you, Abernathy. So follow my lead and don't slow down, or else you'll make a mistake and we'll have to move on without you. And I'm sure your mom won't like that."

I fold my arms. "She could suspend you without even spending a dime," I hiss, and the bratty man smirks.

"I'd be worried if she couldn't. Now get changed. We don't have time to talk about court."

"Here, I'll help you. He can just ... change in the wardrobe or something," Eleanor says, rolling her baby blue eyes.

After Eleanor works her magic, hair and makeup taking only eleven minutes and thirty seconds exactly, I stand in the mirror, fixing hair I didn't know I had. Eleanor curled it nicely and pulled it back into a mid-way ponytail, my hair falling down my back in gentle waves. "What are you, a covert hairdresser?" I ask, glancing back at her.

She smiles. The light sparkles on her cheekbones glittering. "Something like that. You look great, Illiana."

Howard knocks on the door. "Time to go, Eleanor. It's not a fashion show."

"It's close enough!" she grumbles, throwing the door open. "We were done anyways."

Our heels (and dress shoes for Howard, of course) splash in thin puddles along the ground, Eleanor and I grasping our skirts in our hands so as to not stain the fabric. The building is a beautiful, ornate church-looking place, something that could be in a Renaissance painting. Swirling pillars stand out front, guards in black suits and ties carrying two guns underneath their suit coats just outside the doors. Other esteemed guests, dressed up with fine jewelry or combs in their hair, strut in front and behind us, and Howard steps to the back of our group.

An average citizen would think we look like a normal rich group, maybe Eleanor and I coming off as siblings, and Howard being Eleanor's significant other. However, the only reason that he's behind us is to watch for tails and snipers.

Or, more specifically, to watch for the faces that are on the fake IDs. But we're all sort of doing that.

Once we get inside, it becomes more of a waiting game. Guests wander around everywhere, holding drinks from different places of the world. The noise is almost overpowering, but my mother has prepared me well. I can pick out different conversations between guests, like an older French woman talking about where she got her dress, or some Italian describing the newest batch of cannoli he made for his grandmother. There's a curtain at the front of the room, made from genuine red velvet, probably hiding the crown jewels. Two guards, the same as the ones outside, stand at the edges of the curtain. The rest of that half of the room is sectioned off with more velvet rope, curving inwards so no overly curious guest can get a look.

"Split up," Eleanor says quietly, the three of us breaking off in different directions to cover more ground. I scan the crowd, trying to look like a curious American, looking out for the face that looks strangely like me and my mother in the pictures that Howard showed Eleanor and me on the plane.

I have my suspicions. But I don't want to jump to conclusions just yet.

Just when I think there's no way I'm going to find either of them, a young girl with Mom's eyes and blonde hair, strangely matching the pictures, shoves herself into my shoulder, letting out an "Ugh" sound as if I was purposefully in her way.

Just like she totally didn't purposefully shove herself into me.

"I found the girl," I say lowly into my necklace pendant, my earpiece receiving static before Howard's response.

"Good," he says. "Stay on her until the unveiling. Do *not* let her get behind that curtain."

I don't respond, already locked in on the girl as she weaves through the crowd.

Before I can reach her, though, an older man with chestnut brown hair and green eyes smiles, takes my hand, and twirls me around. "Welcome to Monaco, *mon ami!* You are American, yes?"

I nod wordlessly, trying to fake a pleasant expression as I glance over his shoulder. She's gone.

Oh, no.

"Very good, very nice! Have you been enjoying yourself?"

"Oh, yeah, very much!" I stutter, thinking irrationally. "I've even *lost track of the time!*"

I don't need to worry if I said that loud enough, because Howard's voice is in my ear, taking a deep breath. "You *lost* her already, Abernathy?" he hisses.

My eyes catch a flash of blonde hair disappearing behind the curtain, and my heart drops. "Yes, yes, and the food is so good. You could put a *curtain* over my eyes and spoon-feed me, and I wouldn't mind one bit!"

"Great. You let her get to the jewels," Howard mutters.

"Be nice, Howard! She's never been under any pressure like this before, and you're certainly not helping," Eleanor bites back, frustration in her dainty voice.

The man in front of me furrows his brows, and I smile, waving my hand. "It's just an expression we use in America."

"Oh, alright! I agree, then!" I can tell he still has no idea what I'm talking about.

"Thanks for the chat, sir, but I do need to be going. The unveiling is going to be soon. I need to get a good spot."

"Ah, yes. Enjoy Monaco!" he calls after me, but I don't care to look back at him.

"Illiana," Eleanor says breathlessly, her gaze concerned as she studies my face. "Are you alright? Did she do anything bad?"

"No, she just ran into me. Then this guy interrupted me and blocked my path, and I lost her. I'm sorry, I didn't mean to mess things up."

"It's all right," she says, turning her eyes to the curtain. "But I have a feeling we're too late."

A man, probably the Prince of Monaco, stands in front of the curtain, a proud look on his face. "Welcome, everyone!" he says in English, but with a thick French accent. "We are so excited to announce the reveal of the Grimaldi jewels."

His talk becomes background noise as we push through the thickening crowd to get to the rope, a guard waiting for us with an angry look in his eyes.

"If she does try to steal them, wouldn't the alarms go off? That box is so rigged. Something has to go off once she retrieves them," I hiss quietly, Eleanor licking her teeth.

"She's advanced. I've seen her work once before. She knows what she's doing."

I narrow my eyes. "She won't know what to do when she's in prison."

All time seems to stop when the Prince stops talking, our heads turning to the curtain.

The fabric is ripped away, and all of our suspicions are confirmed. I hear Howard's defeated sigh both in the earpiece and in the air, mixing with the astonished gasps and quiet whispers.

"We're too late."

POETRY

Where Did You Go?

Eve Bishop

Grade 10. UNL Independent Study High School, Lincoln, NE.

The sun holds in the rocking distance,
dancing across the ocean to my feet.
Sixty-two days stretch as far as the eye can see,
a wavering distance I cannot reach across.
Where is the end to it?
An ocean holds the sun up,
the same way I see sons bear their fathers' debts.
I want to reach out.
I want to reach that place in the distance.

An endless want hits the water.
Broken promises scattered to the wind like sand, like ashes.
No stop signs, no warnings, no one in the way.
Just a blank chasm.
A chasm I made.
A chasm I tore out with my bare hands, the skin of my palms going raw.
The sun still holds on for dear life as she drowns.
Wavering stars. A wavering distance.
The ocean weeps.
Where did you go?

For your sake,
I cannot hold you any longer.
I cannot find the words to say.

What was I supposed to say?
My mind couldn't keep up.
I couldn't keep up, not when you asked me that.
(Why didn't you tell me?)
Not when you said it like that,
with tears in your eyes, tears in your voice.
What did you want me to say?
What could I have said?
How was I supposed to tell you?
All you could do was cry.
I broke your heart into a million pieces.
How was I supposed to ask for your forgiveness?

A crimson wound stretches sixty-two days across my body.
It tears away at my skin and screams against my rib cage,
longing for something.
Longing for you.
Where is the end to it?

The city sinks into the golden massacre of sun and salt.
I sink further down into the chasm,
into the ocean, into the sunlight,
into the space you used to fill.
A distance I cannot reach dances across the horizon.
The stars lull the waves into an orchestra.
No one hears when I start to drown.
No one hears when my cries bubble away.

For the sake of reaching you,
how much of myself must I give up?
I still search for the parts of me I hid in the palm of your hand,
in the corner of your eyesight,

in the crevice of your heart.
The ocean caved for the sun,
and I caved for you.
The golden light no longer flutters across the water.
Inky colors of the night bleed out in the rocking waves,
a thin line of crimson stretched taut along the horizon.
If I squint, I can still see you.
Dancing. Smiling.
Who did you speak to today?
What do you find happiness in nowadays?
Do you still like the color green and how the mornings look at dawn?
Did I used to make you happy?
(Are you happy?)

The chasm widens. The string tightens. The ocean weeps.

A crimson line. Sixty-two days. Raw skin. A wavering distance.

I want to reach out.

The horizon snaps. The sun is gone. The stars shake.

Where did you go?

ELEANOR THE POET

VICTORIA BOGATZ

Grade 10. Bellevue East Senior High School, Bellevue, NE.

her words spill onto empty pages
creating

how many poems have you written?
I ask
once, at lunch
she answers with a shrug
I don't know
a lot

and I love poems
because it's bending and weaving words
to conjure a feeling
or a memory

eleanor the poet
must like words too
she writes
poems in the breeze

I am a poet now
she says
and she is
because the words don't fail her

she writes
and writes

and I imagine
the adults
and their oft-questioned words
maybe
someday
eleanor
will be a poet

but why must she wait?
the words aren't waiting
eleanor
from b day lunch
and wednesday advisory
is a poet already

and I am too.

Country Life Calls

Katie Bough

Grade 12. Northwest High School, Grand Island, NE.

The dead calf in the creek
The rebar creeping through the crumbling bridge
We see straight through to the stones below
They dump the dead cattle at the end of the avenue
Their bloated bodies stacked in ones and twos
"Off to the glue factory," my mother comically comments
2 miles away
I can't walk down that road
Can't stand the smell
On that road sits the greedy, gloating building that devours the
dead bodies up whole
Where they take the not-so-living livestock
If I dare to bike past it
I clench my teeth
I steel my gaze and stare straight ahead
Focus upon my hands gripping the handlebars
And peddle harder
Pushing past it to get to the sandpits
Where I'll find
Shotgun shells
The carcass of a deer
Antlers off
Broken beer bottles
Crushed cans scattered around or worse

In a pile hidden behind the puzzle pieces of a chopped-down tree, purposely placed to protect someone's secret
When the shotgun sounds
I change my course
Feeling more like prey than a person
Kids across the treeline
My age or older
Fire them into the air
Unaware that bullets don't just disappear
When we drive down gravel roads,
All along the sides are bottles thrown
Out rolled-down windows without a second thought
Empty glass, styrofoam, aluminum
Fastfood takeout boxes, cigarette butts
A reminder
That we matter just that much to them
A place to toss their trash
The people who drive down this road versus the people who live on this road
And guess who picks the rusty nails out of the gravel to keep your tires from popping?

One-Winged

Katie Bough

Grade 12. Northwest High School, Grand Island, NE.

My mind will ne'er let me forget
That wretched one-winged creature

That fought so valiantly
With so much heart
With the full force of spirit
Or the dying decapitation of dread

Fought so bravely against the still evening air, as if it was the wind
that beat him down

Where is the justice in being maimed, not killed?

I can't find it in the lonesome limping turkey, no other feathered
friends in sight for safety
Left to fend for oneself
Abandoned by the flock because her injury endangered them all
She seemed to know she was all alone in the world
That there was nothing left for her but this slow debilitating slope
toward death

The American Nightmare

Ana Brock

Grade 12. Boys Town High School, Boystown, NE.

They see the American Dream
I see the American Nightmare
I see the woman walking miles to work everyday.
I see the man sitting on the street for money because he can't get a job.
I see the young children without parents in the foster system.
I see the man beating the woman because he thinks he's over her.
I see the old man getting put into a mental hospital because no one loves him.
But this is the American Dream, right?
I see the black man always getting accused of stealing just because he is he.
I see the LGBTQ+ community getting hated on because they are expressing themselves.
I see the Muslims not being able to pray during school.
I see the Hispanics always getting asked if they have papers.
But this is the American Dream, right?
I see the street filled with the homeless because the state "cannot" help them.
I see the houses that are broken but still lived in because "nobody can help."
I see all the poor not being able the get anything because the rich already took it.
But this is the American Dream, right?
I see the white man getting away with murder.

I see the mansions and castles build ahead.
I see the white man getting everything he wants just because he can.
I see the white man living.
I see the black man surviving.
But this is the American Dream, right?

Flowers in Life

Ana Brock

Grade 12. Boys Town High School, Boystown, NE.

The life I have lived I can live no more.
The power of my past doesn't hold the chains over me anymore.
I can't sit here and let the thorns poke & stab me anymore.
I have to walk away from those things.
The flowers are the things that hold me together.
They blossom when you least expect and shine when you need them the most.
They help you see the beauty within yourself and the messed up garden we call life.
The past weeds can no longer crawl over my sprouts, I am growing up strong.
Stronger then I have ever been before.
The sun has shown its way through the clouds of my past.
The sun has shown its way to the flowers that have been sitting there waiting for me not to be blind anymore.
The chains aren't there anymore.
The flowers are.
And forever I am thankful.

Forgive Yourself

Ana Brock

Grade 12. Boys Town High School, Boystown, NE.

Forgive yourself for not knowing at the time
Forgive yourself for giving up the power you didn't know you had
Forgive yourself for the past behavior to keep yourself alive
Forgive yourself for the survival patterns you lost on the way
Forgive yourself because you didn't know it wasn't okay
Let your past move on
If you leave it on your shoulders you want to move on
Move on from the dreadful life you lived
Move on from the cycle of unchanged ways
Move on from the hateful words and actions
Always remember
Forgive yourself for who you were and be the person that has always been there but not seen from the naked eye.

The Things That Stay

Ana Brock

Grade 12. Boys Town High School, Boystown, NE.

How do the trees sway?

How do the squirrels run two ways?

How do we not notice them all the
time?

The trees sway and so we walk
along.

The squirrels run so we talk a
poem.

If the trees didn't sway and the
squirrels didn't run

Would we notice?

I don't believe that we would see

The things that are missing even
if we were supposed to.

The leaves crunch underneath the
feet.

But, yet we still don't miss a

beat.

We dream the best when we rest

But, yet we still stay

The trees sway

The squirrels run two ways

We notice them now that we think

Others don't see the things we
shall be

But, the trees still sway

The squirrels still run

Yet we still stay in this restless
mess

So, we don't dream.

How Many More?

Ana Carson

Grade 11. Doniphan-Trumbull High School, Doniphan, NE.
Stacey McCarty, Educator.

How has the world excused genocide?
When are we going to say it's enough?
After 20,000?
50,000?
How many more kids have to die?
Have many more families have to be murdered?
How many more reporters have to be killed?
How many more doctors have to die as martyrs?
They can give as many excuses as they want.
But this is ethnic cleansing.
We are fighting blood with blood in the holy land.
How is that ok?
You want to build schools and malls on the graves of thousands?
Almost 7,000 children have died.
I'm just a child myself.
How am I supposed to see photos of body bags filled with kids the same age as me, and not say anything?
How am I not supposed to be angry?
How many more videos of mothers holding their children's lifeless bodies do I have to watch?
How can we excuse this?
Hospitals have been destroyed.
Schools have been destroyed.
Churches have been destroyed.

What did these innocent people do, to have people saying their homes need to be turned into a “parking lot”?
These people are human.
They bleed red.
They laugh.
They smile.
They love.
And now they are going through hell,
While we watch from the comfort of our homes.

THORN

ANA CARSON

Grade 11. Doniphan-Trumbull High School, Doniphan, NE.
Stacey McCarty, Educator.

I will sit and watch as my walls crumble
While you stand at the center of it all
I'm numb, and you look on as I stumble
But these events I try not to recall

'Cause you may ruin me, but you make me whole
You are my muse, the reason I must wake
You may wreck me, but you unveiled my soul
You will forever be worth the heartache

You can destroy me while I build you up
Call me an architect, a lone creator
Drop me, make me shatter like a teacup
I'll always be your willing partaker

You can be the lust, I'll be the love
You can pick the roses, I'll be the glove

BUBBLEGUM DREAMS

MADALYN CROTEAU

Grade 10. Bellevue West Senior High School, Bellevue, NE.

lain down to rest,
on a marshmallow pillow
traipsing through dreams,
'neath an opalite willow

birds made of candy,
their chirping is sweet,
like silky smooth chocolate
they glide and they tweet

glancing up at the sky,
to see pink fluffy clouds,
cotton candy spun webs,
they hang high and proud

lemonade rivers
with small gummied fish,
rush by rock candy mountains
their tails splash and swish

my bubblegum dreams
drift me soundly to sleep,
counting clusters of fluff,
with wool just like sheep

never shake me awake,
for my heart will be kept
in the place of my childhood,
where i went when i slept

STARRY DREAMS

MADALYN CROTEAU

Grade 10. Bellevue West Senior High School, Bellevue, NE.

my favorite necklace finally broke.
it was a delicate thing,
silver and in the shape of a star.
i wore it everywhere i went
for months on end.
i took it with me and kept
it close to my heart on vacations,
and it saw mountains, rivers,
beaches, waterfalls, lakes, sunrises,
wildflowers;
and as it held those images inside
of its charm, it shone just as bright as
the stars in the sky.
it was my other half, as it saw
me write in my journal, drive my car,
and it reflected the glint in my eye
in a variety of colors as i stood
amongst snow falls and thunderstorms.
it was right by my side when
i cried into my pillow,
catching my sorrows inside of
its 5 small points and holding
them close to my core,
because sad memories are still
memories nonetheless.

it was my everything,
and i forgot it was there most of the time.
so when it finally snapped,
i grabbed it off of my neck and
quietly stood and observed the chain
as it dangled from my fingers.
i then slowly walked toward my bed,
and hung the broken necklace from
a pin holding up my plant poster
i got in salem, remembering
handing the kind worker a handful of coins the
same exact color as the necklace.
now it sits right above my head
when i sleep, and i like to think that
it fills my unconscious mind with starry dreams,
replaying the memories i've experienced
in my time here on earth.
it was a bittersweet moment when
i realized that i broke it by cherishing it
too much.
is my love really that violent?
that destructive, that damaging?
is my love a dying star?
but at the same time,
at least before it starts to fizz out,
it shines memories from within itself.

WHO AM I TO RESIST THE WIND?

MADALYN CROTEAU

Grade 10. Bellevue West Senior High School, Bellevue, NE.

shades of velvet as
deep and as rich
as wine fill the sky,
shining with the moon's
gentle light and glittering
with stars as bright as can be

deer are sleeping soundly
in beds of soft grass with dreams
of prancing through fields,
and raccoons are awake 'neath
the pine trees and oaks,
maples and ashes

wind whispers in my ear,
soft as a hare's fur,
and it tickles my nose with its breeze.
it begins to beckon me,
pull me, lead me
away from all of my sorrows

it's telling me to leave everything
behind, and instead, sleep under
the night sky and eat fresh berries
for breakfast by the flowing streams,

allow the mountains and wildflowers
and rain to take me in with open arms

and who am i to resist the wind?

Old Mrs. Mae

Claire Davis

Grade 11. Hastings Senior High School, Hastings, NE.

Your skin has thinned to blushing rose petals
That turn to dust in the breeze
If I were to brush up against you by accident
You would disintegrate
Slowly
With both madness and enchantment

The stillness in your eyes is unbearable
Not even Atlas and his weary quaking could move your gaze
But I suppose you two are one and the same
His shift is ending and you must return to waltzing with the world
 on your frail shoulders

The tremors flowing through your veins and resting in your hands
Are like the whisper-screams of the wise
Cataclysmically moving sleeping tectonic plates

The drying brush of your mind has caught fire
Destruction is having its heyday
Memories fading away from your glassy mind

The Whitecoats say it's not sad, they say it's deterioration
They prick and they poke
With every harsh move of their needle-like steel blue hands
You fade back into the foggy distance of your skull

They wear blue chemical skins to hide the cold washers and screws
that lie in wait beneath
To shield their inner mechanics from the sticky tears that fall
throughout the hospital
It seems it's raining
Even when you first enter, the weight of barren consequence is cast
upon you

All this messy grey chaos is clouding around my head
And percolating stiffly
Still, I zero in on your wandering soul
I can hear its ebb and flow in the prosthetic finger they leeched on
you
It's slowing
You're leaving me

And just like that
—You're gone

Daydreams

Darbie deFreese

Grade 9. Holdrege High School, Holdrege, NE.

Darkness is my blank canvas
The perfect portrait for my dreams
Painted with the colors of my world
Yet it still remains pitch black

Songs of wonder fuel my desires
Pulling me through fields of joy
Pushing me through forests of woe
Providing tales to fill my mind

Ink absorbs my thoughts
Shadows shift to paint
Rainbows stain my clothes
Everything halts conscience

My shirt fades to blue
My pants turn to red
My glasses shine pink
My shoes darken green

Color soaks up my breath and being
Ideas burn into my lungs and soul
Words enclose my neck and mind
Stories freeze my throat and heart

A faraway light falls down on me
Comforting me in a faithful love
Condoling me with tender words
Carrying me attentively home

I return quietly to my reality
Apprehensively, I dot it with blue
Then yellow, then red, then green
Real and warm and passionate
I find myself, doused in life

The Garden

Kimmy Findeis

Grade 12. Millard West High School, Omaha, NE.

"Ashes to ashes, dust to dust,"
Repeat those who have fallen at the feet of their lust,
Who lured them to the shadows at such a callow state,
Reigning down upon their heads their formidable fate.
For a moment of bliss is there too big a wage?
To enter what once was a garden in the midst of a cage?
For what sweet succulent fruit it bore,
Extending its arm through an open door.
In a plight amongst the figures of dark and light,
Where the bright come entangled in a dull grim gray,
Floating round in a mindless daze.
As once cold dark spirits may rise to new heights,
In hopes to be greeted by the pearly gates of eternal life.

Strung Together

Ainsley LaHolt

Grade 11. Lincoln Southwest High School, Lincoln, NE.

Here it is!
A gift for you!
Something I meticulously—
Slaved over for hours,
Wishing for the moment
To give it—
And you,
Passed it around,
Like you didn't. even. know.

I want to try.
To look them in the eyes and say
"I love you."

At times, it's more difficult.
Sometimes, I'm pulling an invisible string,
In the back of my throat,
The words just falling out.

But maybe that's love.

Maybe tugging on that string
Shows how willing you are,
How far you would go,
How *deep* your love truly *is.*

So,

I pull on that string,
Time and time again,
No matter how much it cuts,
those words that are really in the back of my throat,

Because,
"I love you"
Are just words,
They aren't actually supposed to mean anything.
It's the effort that comes with actually
Saying it,
Even when you really don't mean it.
Even when you wish you could say the opposite,
Because while the former keeps a smile on their face,
The latter loosens the string—

—*It's just words,*
They don't *actually* mean anything.

Because if you think about it for too long,
You realize,
That maybe it really isn't love,
Maybe just the calm that comes with the repetition,
The safety that it'll be given back,
Even if,
they feel the same—
Because at the end of the day,
The words
"I love you"
And

"I tolerate you"
Are *gifts;*
Tied with the same string.

And I Tell Her

Magnolia Moriarty

Grade 10. Millard South High School, Omaha, NE.

I had strep throat last May.
The first time I've ever had it.
When the doctor called my name,
Lead me into the white brick room
with a poster of the alphabet as diseases
They asked me for my symptoms.
And my lungs told me not to speak.
I couldn't speak.
My voice was lost underneath layers of phlegm
Behind these white brick walls
With a poster of the alphabet as diseases,
I couldn't speak.
When I was in the fifth grade my anxiety set in.
In a matter of months, I had gone from the
Friendliest kid you'd meet to wearing long sleeves in 90-degree heat
Because I was already scared of what people would think of my body.
I was already scared of people.
I tried to make friends but it was too late,
The fears had already made their homes
Ready to stay.
I couldn't disappoint the guests.
I couldn't speak.
A few days ago I finished my bottle of
soap at the same time as my shampoo.

And so I gathered up my cash
And I drove to the store.
Yesterday I wanted to take an eternal nap
And so I set my alarm for twenty minutes
Because time doesn't matter anymore
When you want to take every last second away from you
Today no one spoke kindly to me.
And so tonight,
I will tell myself all the words I have never spoken.
I saw a girl in the grocery store with gorgeous red hair,
And I told her so.
There is a man at work who always wears
Funny socks, and I told him I liked them.
There is a boy I love dearly who no one ever spoke kindly to
And I tell him I love him.
I see the girl with dark hair,
The one who waves at every dog she sees.
I see the girl with yellowed teeth and crow's feet and lines when she smiles.
I see her and I smile.
I brush her dark hair and yellowed teeth,
And tell her all the words never spoken.
I couldn't speak.
Once.
But now I can tell her that it's going to be okay.

THE POET'S EYE

MAGNOLIA MORIARTY

Grade 10. Millard South High School, Omaha, NE.

I want to look at the world
The way a poet looks at his words.
I want to see everything
With the fighting beauty and sadness it holds
And I want the things I create,
To be looked at the same.

I want to see the world
The way an artist sees their work.
Understanding the story within
Seeing everything around me as something
And I want the things I create
To be looked at the same.

But
Sometimes I dream of being an admirer
And not the poet.
Appreciate the world for all its drifts and flows
And not needing to have
A metaphor to show how it relates to something deeper.

But sometimes
Sometimes I dream of no longer being the poet,
No longer being the artist, no longer human at all.

And instead the poem, the art, the beauty.
Beauty enough to be someone's passion.

To Anyone Who Wants to Love Me

Katelyn Omer

Grade 9. Millard North High School, Omaha, NE.

To anyone who wants to love me
you cannot steal my heart
because I have
stolen it back from endless quicksands
and rescued it from the depths of the sea
I've saved it from hell
watched it swell
with love I fed myself
I've nourished it back to health
No, no one can steal my heart
because it is mine
But if you knock gently on its door
I might let you in for a time

To anyone who wants to love me
you cannot own my body
because I know it's priceless
Only I have looked admiringly
towards the scars on the wall
I was the first one to love
my curves and stretch marks
so they will forever be loyal to me
No good looks or cute guys or emotional rides
can pull me away from my boundaries
because not everyone deserves to walk in the garden of me

But if you're willing to stay for eternity
I'll show you a gentle grace you've never before seen

To anyone who wants to love me
you cannot take credit for my healing
Boys are not bandaids
I will ever rely on to fix me
I have fought blood and knife
to still be alive and now I thrive
Do you see me thrive?
I cannot afford to lose the pride
I have in my progress
but if you applaud it
I will let you stay long enough to see
how I always turn my ashes to beauty

To anyone who doesn't want to love me
I don't need you to
Did you hear me? I don't need you too
I sing those words because they ring of freedom
Waiting for others' approval is a crutch
I'm finally leaving in the dust
Watch me fly for the first time
It's a long road that leads here
but if you follow it, grow in self love,
you will reach above, above ... to freedom

Icarus

Jay Peters

Grade 11. Omaha South High Magnet School, Omaha, NE.

I've seen you crafting your wings
Millions of miles below me
Your fingers deft, knitting together
A skeleton of wax
Nestled in downy feathers
They cling to your skin
Like a blanket of hopes and dreams
So soft under your touch
You plan your flight to me
To the light in your sky
You don't see the danger
Nor do you see my scalding heat
You know that I'll burn you
And that I'll melt the fragile bones
That take you to the sky
You need to go down to earth
I want you to be safe
And to be safe
You need to stay away
It isn't that I don't want you
God, I want you more than anything
But I'll hurt you
Liquefy the wings of your love
And send you plummeting to the sea
I don't want you to drown

And I know you can't swim to shore
So stay, my love
Stay on the land
Where you're safe and comfortable
Abandon your wings
Build yourself a life down below
And while I can't hold you
I'll warm your skin from above
And pray that's enough

Folie à Deux

Lilly Pfeilsticker

Grade 12. Fort Calhoun Junior Senior High School, Fort Calhoun, NE. Sara Gross, Educator.

In the night,
Fingers intertwined so tightly
Bones ache against each other
through purpling skin
The world is cold
Hands around each others' necks,
woven together
like chainmail scarfs
In your grasp, I'll stay

In time, the dawn comes
Our hands relax
and natural color returns to our finger tips.
Looser and looser
they become.
You notice.
I noticed some time ago.
Why did you let go?
I do not want to answer.
Because it is not the night anymore. The monsters have gone.

But did we not fight the monsters together?

I suppose so, but the night is done and,

I have grown so tired of clinging.

TAROT

SAM ROGERS

Grade 10. Hastings Senior High School, Hastings, NE.

changing like the wheel of fortune
i want to tear off this skin
and replace it with something new
something as good as you

i want to pay attention
but my thoughts cloud my vision
i'll rip them to pieces
and shove all my teeth back in

i'm afraid i'm just something to spare
one day someone will walk on my back
my spine will crack
but at least that vision will be clear

THE FISHERMAN

PRISCILLA TON

Grade 11. North Star High School, Lincoln, NE.

If this is the only reason I am alive,
Then a person would be likely to think that it is awfully cruel.

Think diligently: of midnight and a rocking ship at sea
Imagine the breaths of rampant waves that incessantly call your name
The cold creeping in; the beating of a rising panic,
Knocking incessantly against the bones of your breast

Recall, if you are able, from this life, or a life past,
An exhale of repose as a beam of the lighthouse catches on your eyelids, and solace may settle
The duty of a fisherman to fish is an awfully fickle venture
We throw our day's work in buckets overboard—the price that must be paid to go home.

Turned over boats and gasping breaths,
Desperate reaching and flailing arms
Planets, that are ever so divergent, coexist, and transpire;
And innately orbit around our lighthouse.

This is the only reason I am alive: to spend my days out at sea and suffer,
To be indebted to the lighthouse, and to persist in eternal servitude.

A Fine Wine

Cassandra Wong

Grade 12. Millard South High School, Omaha, NE.

I used to sparkle
A bright bubbled champagne
I was the life of the party
The glitz and the glam
But somewhere in the haze
That drunk foggy line
I simply became
An aged bottle of wine

Some days I pour
an easy cheap box
I pour so stupidly
Into styrofoam cups
But some days I exist
In the cellars below
Hidden far beneath
And coated in dust

I exist in the cellar
Corked and untouched
Because what is my flavor,
My worth,
For just what am I worth
If popped open so rudely?

What am I worth if I
Pour out for just any?

The Swamp

Cassandra Wong

Grade 12. Millard South High School, Omaha, NE.

this murky green water glides upon a bare back
trees glitter with sun,
shadows pass by, covering bits in a quiet black
dimming and brightening, it's a land for no ordinary son

trees glitter with sun,
and sweat is slick on skin
dimming and brightening, it's a land for no ordinary son
when it's over, he'll grunt, and flash you a grin

and sweat is slick on skin
my wooded hollow,
when it's over, he'll grunt, and flash you a grin
this slow heated grotto.

my wooded hollow
it no longer gives me peace
this slow heated grotto
just a place for his release

it no longer gives me peace
his hands in mine,
just a place for his release
a swamp for bodies to twine.

his hands in mine,
shadows pass by, covering his fits in quiet black
a swamp for bodies to twine.
and this green water glides upon our bare backs

CRITICAL ESSAY

The Art of Teaching

Taylor Beierman

Grade 12. Boone Central High School, Albion, NE.

Dating back to ancient civilizations, education has continued to be the essential root that has constructed the foundation of societies around the globe. While strategies for teaching have evolved, the objective of assisting students' learning experience has remained the same. In the last twenty years, however, the United States has obsessed over one methodology for education: teaching to the test. As mentioned by Jennings and Bearak in *"Teaching to the Test" in the NCLB Era* (2014), since the enactment of the No Child Left Behind Act of 2001, states have conducted annual standardized tests in grades three through twelve, measuring student academic achievement. While some argue that teaching to the test has improved standardized exam results and closed the achievement gap, there are significant deficiencies in the strategic process. Due to inaccuracies in standardized tests, psychological effects on teachers and students, and a decline in creative thinking skills, teaching to the test methods in secondary education systems is far more risky than rewarding.

While standardized testing is prominent and widely used across the United States, it fails to measure student learning and growth efficiently. In a school-wide survey I conducted in November 2023, forty random high school students were asked if they believed standardized tests accurately measure their intelligence. Ninety percent of those asked responded, "No, the tests are flawed and don't show my true abilities." Likewise, numerous students are inefficient test takers. Some may experience anxiety, while others simply freeze up and lack critical thinking skills. Following an in-depth interview with thirty-five-year high school veteran teacher Mr. Dan Zoucha, it is clear that standardized tests fail to show what a student genuinely knows (personal interview, November 2, 2023). While some argue that standardized tests help educators determine what their students know or have learned, Zoucha points out that in his experience, standardized exams, such as MAPS testing and the ACT, only measure how well a student can take that test (Zoucha, personal interview, November 2, 2023). In many instances, students who received lower scores on standardized assessments, such as the ACT, still graduated college with above-average grades. Conversely, some students who scored high on standardized tests failed to complete their post-secondary education. In other words, standardized tests simply do not accurately estimate a student's future success. Not only do standardized assessments ineffectively measure a student's subsequent achievement, but they also lack sufficient data analysis and accuracy. According to the National Center for Education Statistics (2023), "the overall college enrollment rate for 18 to 24-year-olds decreased from 41 percent in 2010 to 38 percent in 2021" (p. 1). In the State of Nebraska, all juniors are required to take the ACT regardless of whether or not they attend college. As a result, some students refrain from laboring on the exam. Consequently, a percentage of standardized assessments is inaccurate. As revealed by Anya Kamenetz (2016), a GAO (Government Accountability Office) report in 2013 states that "officials in 32 states canceled, invalidated, or nullified test scores as a result of cheating" (p. 2). Nonetheless, out of the millions of standardized tests taken each year by students in the United States, the odds of additional instances of academic dishonesty that get missed are high. In a comprehensive interview with one Nebraska high school mathematics teacher, Mr. Jeffrey Hrabik, he spotlighted the illuminating unknowns that come with each standardized test as questions differentiate each year (personal interview, November 2, 2023).

Hrabik noted an obstacle in ascertaining the growth of knowledge in students that can be attributed to considerable score fluctuation from year to year (personal interview, November 2, 2023). Too much attention on standardized tests that are inaccurate representations of students' learning abilities leads to wasted time on exam-based curricula.

In light of obstacles manufactured from teaching to the test, it is important to note the psychological impact of high-stakes testing cultures in schools on educators. Smit, Lesley, Baker, & Stewart (2022) argue, "Teachers who live in fear of their schools being reconstituted and losing their jobs feel pressure to teach to the test" (p. 3). The assumption that inflated test scores will deem a school successful can be a dangerous form of reasoning. To gain an inside perspective on what pressures secondary educators face today, Miss Cassandra Olson, a high school English and History teacher, explained the persistent battle inside teachers' minds between tackling state standards efficiently and exerting more emphasis on topical reflection (personal interview, November 3, 2023). Many, ultimately, choose to eliminate essential curricular content that is not included in the test (Olson, personal interview, November 3, 2023). Dr. Louis Volante (2004) proclaims, "Teaching to the test only serves to exacerbate feelings of frustration and disillusionment with the entire testing process" (p. 2). Furthermore, teacher shortages are growing across the country. Overall, education staff have become increasingly despondent with the narrowed focus on teaching standardized tests.

In the same fashion, teaching to the test can substantially impact students' emotional stress and anxiety. In the same survey as mentioned earlier, 87.5% of students experienced some form of anxiety from standardized tests, with 40% of those who said yes suffering high amounts of nerves and uneasiness. Countless students face exceeding volumes of urgency due to teaching to the test methods. Thirty-four out of forty students articulated an increased amount of pressure to perform well on standardized tests. Of those thirty-four, 55.6% said they felt pressure from their parents, 44.4% from teachers, 11.2% from peers, and an incredible 86.1% felt pressure from themselves. Strikingly, one student commented feeling influenced by older siblings' high performances. Emotionally, students may feel intimidated by classmates or left behind due to subordinate test scores. All in all, emphasis on standardized tests has disastrous consequences for high school students.

As teaching to the test strategies have expanded over recent years, creative thinking skills, conversely, have condensed beyond an admissible degree of expectation with a shift in quality instruction. As highlighted in the *High School Journal*, studies show that most instruction in current classrooms is "monologic, meaning that teachers dominate instruction ... so that students have little opportunity to influence the course of the class session" (Gamoran & Carbonaro, 2002, pp. 1–2). Straightforward thinking limits the development of students' expressive abilities. "Dialogic" instruction, however, exceeds the conventional initiation-response-evaluation of instruction to empower a more conversational exchange among students and educators (Gamoran & Carbonaro, 2002). Undoubtedly, while aiming to cover the test, it becomes arduous for educators to decelerate and force a dialogic approach encouraging students to think critically. Gamoran and Carbonaro (2002) illustrate that, "sustained classroom discussion ... stimulates modes of cognition (thinking and not just remembering) that differ from those of recitation" (p. 2). Correlative communication in classrooms forces educators to step away from teaching to the test, inevitably elevating the development of students' critical thinking.

Comparatively, assessment practices presented through specific teacher goal structures diminish student creativity and skill development. Beghetto's journal article, "Does Assessment Kill Student

Creativity" (2005), classified educators' goal-related messages into two categories: performance-goal structures and mastery-goal structures. "A performance goal structure is represented by goal-related messages that stress the importance of avoiding mistakes, besting others, getting the highest grades, and demonstrating one's ability in relation to others" (Beghetto, 2005, p. 4). In this format, students are encouraged to dominate classmates, facilitating an increase in their anxiety levels. Observational evidence suggests that students in performance-goal structures "are more likely to view errors as an indication of a lack of ability, experience high levels of anxiety, exert less effort, place less value on tasks, and give up in the face of difficulty" (Beghetto, 2005, p. 5). While an emphasis on improving standardized test scores using a performance structure may solve the issue of low test achievement, it presents new challenges for teachers to correct the shortfalls created in the process.

In every inch of the world, education is the centerpiece of imagination and encouragement of individuals' overall productivity in society. Unfortunately, teaching to the test techniques are being implemented in classrooms to educate students. While this may inflate standardized exam achievement, the underlying consequences are detrimental. As a result, teaching to the test methods in secondary education systems are far more risky than rewarding due to inaccuracies in standardized tests, psychological effects on teachers and students, and a decline in creative thinking skills. From first-hand student input to experienced educators' viewpoints, it is evident that teaching to the test, inevitably, does no good for all individuals involved. Education must be restructured to alleviate pressure on instruction and instead preserve enjoyment in learning something new in class. As American poet and writer, Mark Van Doren, put it best, "The art of teaching is the art of assisting discovery."

References

Beghetto, R. A. (2005). Does Assessment Kill Student Creativity? *The Educational Forum*, 69(3), 254–263. https://doi.org/10.1080/00131720508984694

Gamoran, A., & Carbonaro, W. J. (2002). High School English: A National Portrait. *High School Journal*, 86(2), 1. https://doi.org/10.1353/hsj.2002.0021

Jennings, J., & Bearak, J. (2014). "Teaching to the Test" in the NCLB Era: How Test Predictability Affects Our Understanding of Student Performance. *Educational Researcher*, 43(8), p. 381. https://doi.org/10.3102/0013189X14554449

Kamenetz, A. (2016). The Problem with Testing. *Saturday Evening Post*, 288(5), 10–80.

National Center for Education Statistics. (2023). College Enrollment Rates. *Condition of Education*. U.S. Department of Education, Institute of Education Sciences. https://nces.ed.gov/programs/coe/indicator/cpb.

Smit, J., Lesley, M., Baker, B. W., & Stewart, E. (2022). Investigating Meaningful Impact in Adolescent Writing Achievement Within a High-stakes Testing Context. *Journal of Research in Reading*, 45(3), 447–467. https://doi.org/10.1111/1467-9817.12397

Volante, L. (2004). Teaching to the Test: What Every Educator and Policy-Maker Should Know. *Canadian Journal of Educational Administration and Policy*, 35, 1–6. ERIC. https://eric.ed.gov/?q=test+preparation&ff1=dtySince_2004&ff2=subStandardized+Tests&ff3=pubJournal+Articles&ff4=pubReports+-+Descriptive&ff5=lawNo+Child+Left+-Behind+Act+2001&id=EJ848235

Growing Up in a World That's Falling Apart

A Look at Climate Anxiety

Victoria Bogatz

Grade 10. Bellevue East Senior High School, Bellevue, NE.
Trish Swoboda, Educator.

This summer, the record for the hottest day in Earth's recorded history was broken—four days in a row (Jacobo). In a 2021 heat wave in the Salish Sea, billions of small sea creatures boiled alive (White et al.). 2020 tied 2016 for the hottest year on record ("Vital Signs: Global Temperature"). Currently, one million species are at risk of extinction (Manning and Ingram).

Facts like these are enough to send anyone into an anxious spiral. Climate change is real, and not only is it devastating our planet, but it is also affecting the mental health of people worldwide. According to Yale University, 64% of Americans are at least somewhat worried about climate change, while around 27% say they are *very* worried ("Yale Experts Explain Climate Anxiety"). This climate-related stress is often referred to as eco- or climate anxiety.

Climate anxiety is completely valid, but when this distress starts to paralyze people, it can become a problem. If the fear of climate change consumes you, if your well of hope runs dry, then climate action may seem meaningless. If a better future is impossible, why work towards one?

However, a better future is always possible. Climate anxiety doesn't have to stall action. In fact, it can propel it.

Anxiety about the environment is caused by multiple factors and has negative effects on physical and mental health. However, there are many ways to combat climate anxiety and help the environment, including collective activism. Climate change may seem hopeless, but it's when we learn to turn our fear into action that we can change the world.

Concern about climate change has been studied for decades, but the term "climate anxiety" is relatively new. Psychologist and professor Sarah Lowe defines climate anxiety as: "Distress about climate change and its impacts on the landscape and human existence" ("Yale Experts").

In recent years, climate anxiety has escalated. According to the news outlet Grist, Google searches for "climate anxiety" increased by 565 percent in 2021 (qtd. in "Yale Experts"). This increase in climate anxiety may be fueled by the worsening of the climate crisis itself. As humans burn fossil fuels, releasing greenhouse gasses into the atmosphere, our planet continues to warm. Extreme weather and devastating natural disasters around the world have made the dangers of climate change clearer than ever.

The climate crisis is not some distant, terrifying future. Climate change is happening right here, right now. However, it may feel like it has snuck up on us. When did scientists' desperate warnings of 2010 become the destructive natural disasters of 2020? We cannot go on living our lives, tied to the status quo while our environment falls apart. We *must* act on climate change, a message that scientists and journalists have been pushing for years. But while scientists tend to stick to the cold, hard facts, the press can be more dramatic—producing doomsday news reports to scare people into action.

For example, the Intergovernmental Panel on Climate Change has created a goal of stopping an increase in global temperatures at 1.5 degrees Celsius (Allen et al.). However, the media has interpreted this as sort of a tipping point (Osaka)—that if we reach 1.5 degrees Celsius of warming, that's it. It's over.

The truth is, the planet has already warmed by about 1.1 degrees since the pre-industrial period ("Vital Signs"). We are already experiencing climate change every day ("The Effects of Climate Change"). This 1.5 degrees is simply a goal to hold governments and corporations accountable. The news has taken it to the next level, producing the scariest stories possible to inspire the public into action.

This doesn't always work. Additionally, the message of encouraging climate action is often contradicted by companies and those in power who wish to delay climate action. This dichotomy can be exhausting.

Between extreme weather, scary news reports, and conflicting messages, it's no wonder that 59% of youth feel very or extremely worried about climate change, according to a study published in *Lancet Planetary Health* (Hickman et al.). This fear about climate change, an issue that seems so out of anyone's control, often leaves those with climate anxiety feeling stuck. Uncertain of solutions, one's anxiety may simply spiral.

The effects of climate anxiety can be serious. In the same study by Hickman et al., approximately 45% of youth said that stress about climate change impacts their day-to-day lives. Not every young person does care about climate change, but for many, fears about the worsening climate crisis leave them wondering how to grow up in a world that's falling apart.

It's not only youth. Anxiety can be debilitating for people of all ages, whether it's caused by the climate or other issues. Anxiety can arise over any issue, but distress specifically about the environment is what sets climate anxiety apart. Physical anxiety can present itself through sweating, trembling, a raised heart rate, gastrointestinal issues, or tiredness. Mental effects include trouble focusing, a persistent sense of danger or panic, and difficulty controlling worry ("Anxiety Disorders"). Clearly, anxiety is not good. Over time, the negative effects of climate anxiety can take their toll, leaving one feeling stuck or hopeless.

Those with climate anxiety aren't making the choice to be concerned about the environment, either. In a 2020 interview with the New York Times, teen climate activist Jamie Margolin said that she wished she didn't have to worry about the climate crisis. She expressed frustration that adults haven't taken care of the issue, leaving her and other teenagers to fight for change (Jarvis).

Margolin ended up in activism. But at first, she simply didn't know what to do about climate change—like many others. According to a report by Carbon Majors, just 100 fossil fuel companies are responsible for 71% of global industrial carbon emissions (Griffin). Statistics like these make it seem as though climate change is a distant, complex issue. It may feel like all one can do is sit by and watch it happen.

Securing a livable future does depend on whether governments and corporations take the necessary action to stop the climate crisis. However, that doesn't mean individual climate action is futile. Additionally, research shows that *collective* climate activism is not only a force for change, but it can also drastically improve climate-related anxiety.

I mentioned activist Jamie Margolin. Another young climate advocate—arguably one of the most famous—was propelled into climate action by her depression and hyper-fixation on climate change. Of course, this would be Greta Thunberg.

In 2018, Thunberg began her "school strike for the climate" movement as a young teen, depressed and feeling alone in her concern for the environment. Now, her school strike movement has spread to 71 countries, and Thunberg has spoken before the United Nations (Watts).

Imagine if everyone with climate anxiety channeled their worry into just a *fraction* of the climate activism of Greta Thunberg. I think we could change the world.

And change is happening. Slowly but surely, as climate action has increased, the climate crisis is becoming a more prominent issue in the eye of the general public. In the 2012 presidential debate, climate change was not discussed at all, but in the 2020 election, environmental issues were major campaign points for many candidates (Jarvis). In 2022, Congress passed the Inflation Reduction Act, described by the Environmental Protection Agency as "the most significant climate legislation in U.S. history" ("Summary of Inflation Reduction Act provisions related to renewable energy"). It's difficult to measure the direct effects of any activist movement. However, the correlation between a blossoming climate movement and increased discussion of and action on the issue is clear.

Not only does climate action contribute to positive change, it has been proven to ease climate anxiety. A national study by Yale University found that young adults with climate anxiety who were involved in collective activism had fewer symptoms of depression than those who did *not* participate in activism. Climate action gives people hope— but more specifically, *collective* action.

While simple individual actions to help the environment, such as driving less or planting trees, are important, the Yale study found that they were not very effective in easing climate anxiety. Collective action, on the other hand—such as community outreach, raising awareness about the environment, or joining advocacy groups—is far more powerful (Schwartz et al.). Individual actions like recycling may feel insignificant in the grand scheme of things ("Yale Experts"). The results of systemic climate action are far more tangible. You don't know how the plastic bottles you recycle will be remade. But if, say, a petition that you sign leads a senator to sponsor an environmental bill, you begin to *witness* the effects of your action firsthand.

Also, collective action connects those with climate anxiety to a *community*. Finding like-minded people can teach you that you are not alone in caring about the environment (Fine), which is almost as powerful as any climate action you will ever take.

It is important to remember that anxiety has no easy cure. There's no shame in being anxious, but if your anxiety feels out of control or is interfering with your everyday life, experts recommend seeking help from a doctor or mental health provider ("Anxiety Disorders"). Collective activism can ease climate anxiety, but it is no substitute for professional help.

On the other hand, many people do not understand the widespread distress over climate change. For those who are not concerned about the environment, it is important to remember that the climate crisis is affecting everyone on our planet. Adverse impacts of climate change include rising sea levels, increased heat waves, droughts, wildfires, floods, and more ("The Effects of Climate Change"). Do we want to live in a world where it's no longer safe to be outdoors? Where humans are destroying the very environment that has kept us alive for thousands of years? We can't all succumb to climate anxiety and doomism, but we must recognize the severity of the climate crisis if we are to act on it.

Anxiety about the environment is widespread and has negative effects on both physical and mental health. However, climate action—especially collective activism—is one of the best ways to combat anxiety and make a difference.

Whether climate anxiety keeps you up at night, or you couldn't care less about the environment, everyone can and should act on climate change. Act on an individual level: buy locally, save energy around your home, or use less plastic. Most importantly, bring your climate action to a bigger scale by voting for candidates who care about climate change, joining a local organization dedicated to protecting the environment, or writing to your elected officials urging them to take action on the climate crisis.

Maybe activism is scary, but climate change is scarier. Frankly, we can't wait any longer to take action. It's time to face our worries. It's time to change the world.

Works Cited

Allen, Myles R., et al. "Summary for Policymakers." *Global Warming of 1.5°C: An IPCC Special Report on the impacts of global warming of 1.5°C above pre-industrial levels and related global greenhouse gas emission pathways, in the context of strengthening the global response to the threat of climate change, sustainable development, and efforts to eradicate poverty*, 6 Oct. 2018, https://doi.org/10.1017/9781009157940.001.

"Anxiety Disorders." *Mayo Clinic*, 4 May 2018, www.mayoclinic.org/diseases-conditions/anxiety/symptoms-causes/syc-20350961.

"The Effects of Climate Change." *Global Climate Change,* edited by Holly Shaftel et al., National Aeronautics and Space Administration, climate.nasa.gov/effects/.

Fine, Julia. "*5 Ways* Climate Activism Could Make You Happier." *Teen Vogue*, 4 Dec. 2019, www.teenvogue.com/story/climate-change-activist-how-get-involved.

Griffin, Paul. "The Carbon Majors Database: CDP Carbon Majors Report 2017." *Carbon Disclosure Project*, July 2017, cdn.cdp.net/cdp-production/cms/reports/documents/000/002/327/original/Carbon-Majors-Report-2017.pdf.

Hickman, Caroline, et al. "Climate Anxiety in Children and Young People and Their Beliefs about Government Responses to Climate Change: A Global Survey." *Lancet Planetary Health*, vol. 5, no. 12, 8 Dec. 2021, https://doi.org/10.15125/BATH-01124. Abstract.

Jacobo, Julia. "Earth Reaches Hottest Day Ever Recorded 4 Days in a Row." *ABC News*, 7 July 2023, abcnews.go.com/

US/4th-july-breaks-record-highest-temperature-measured/story?id=100702850.

Jarvis, Brooke. "The Teenagers at the End of the World." *The New York Times Magazine*, 21 July 2020, www.nytimes.com/interactive/2020/07/21/magazine/teenage-activist-climate-change.html.

Manning, Jonathan, and Simon Ingram. "26 Facts That Bring Home the Reality of Climate Change." *National Geographic*, 30 Oct. 2021, www.nationalgeographic.co.uk/26facts.

Osaka, Shannon. "Why Climate 'Doomers' Are Replacing Climate 'Deniers.'" *Washington Post*, 23 Mar. 2023, www.washingtonpost.com/climate-environment/2023/03/24/climate-doomers-ipcc-un-report/.

Schwartz, Sarah E. O., et al. "Climate Change Anxiety and Mental Health: Environmental Activism as Buffer." *Current Psychology*, vol. 42, July 2023, https://doi.org/10.1007/s12144-022-02735-6.

"Summary of Inflation Reduction Act Provisions Related to Renewable Energy." *United States Environmental Protection Agency*, www.epa.gov/green-power-markets/summary-inflation-reduction-act-provisions-related-renewable-energy#:~:text=The%20Inflation%20Reduction%20Act%20of,of%20new%20clean%20electricity%20resources.

"Vital Signs: Global Temperature." *Global Climate Change*, edited by Holly Shaftel et al., National Aeronautics and Space Administration, climate.nasa.gov/vital-signs/global-temperature/.

Watts, Johnathan. "Greta Thunberg, Schoolgirl Climate Change Warrior: 'Some People Can Let Things Go. I Can't.'" *The Guardian*, 11 Mar. 2019, www.theguardian.com/world/2019/mar/11/greta-thunberg-schoolgirl-climate-change-warrior-some-people-can-let-things-go-i-cant.

White, Rachel H., et al. “The Unprecedented Pacific Northwest Heatwave of June 2021.” *Nature Communications*, vol. 14, 9 Feb. 2023, https://www.nature.com/articles/s41467-023-36289-3#citeas.

“Yale Experts Explain Climate Anxiety.” *Yale Sustainability*, Yale University, 13 Mar. 2023, sustainability.yale.edu/explainers/yale-experts-explain-climate-anxiety.

PERSONAL ESSAY & MEMOIR

Inside the Glass Gallery

Jocelyn Huang

Grade 11. Millard North High School, Omaha, NE.

I blink down emptily looking at my clammy hands, now trickling with sweat droplets. Every crevice of my trembling fingertips and nails is now covered in dark, merciless ink—my mouth stings like the sour taste of black licorice jellybeans. The classroom, in contrast, is full of bustling life and children's laughter. One could enter this room and describe this scene as a pinnacle moment of creativity, a glimpse of hope for the future generation. The teacher, my mama, raised the project made by my best friend. To this, the class roared with praise and applause. The project consisted of a singular white sheet of paper, lined meticulously with glue, on top of a larger, purple construction paper. On the white paper, a sakura cherry blossom tree sprung to life. Although this trivial art project seemed like just another checkmark to cross off on the curriculum list for the Mandarin Level II class, only one thought flooded my mind when I saw the project: it was beautiful.

The instructions were quite simple. First, place a droplet of black ink onto the white piece of paper. Secondly, rotate the paper downwards to allow the ink to run down and create the trunk of the cherry blossom, blowing gently outwards on the clumps of ink to create smaller branches, and repeatedly to create the twigs that grew on the branches. This step, however, baffled me. My first tree's black ink had run right off of my paper, leaving me no choice but to restart rather than work with the ridiculously tall trunk. After a second and third attempt, my tree's branches grew too much and sank the entire tree. The mix of Elmer's glue and jet-black ink resembled a hybrid

Cow's spots or melted Oreo ice-cream slush. On my fourth attempt, my tree's branches refused to grow. Out of a moment of impulsive frustration, I blew all the air from my lungs, sacrificing every ounce of hope in me, desperate for my tree to bloom. My stubborn tree refused to comply and instead, its black inky blood shot onto my lips. I looked around the paper garden of all my other classmates' trees, each one dutifully growing so fruitfully. Each tree had a sturdy trunk and perfectly balanced branches that cradled detailed twigs. Light-blushing sakura flowers, as dainty as crumpled tissue paper, sprouted out of each twig. I had inadvertently killed my tree and would never see it blossom. My tree would be cursed to live an eternal winter. As the realization hit and my eyes began to swim with tears, I burst out of the classroom, ran to the restroom, and locked myself in a stall. In a courtyard full of accomplished gardeners I couldn't even plant a seed. In a classroom of gifted artists, I could merely doodle.

When I eventually convinced myself to walk out of the restroom, after cleansing my hands of my cherry blossom's ink-stained blood, the class had already ended. I found my mama hanging up the rest of my classmates' trees inside the glass gallery. All the paintings together made a 3x5 square shape behind the glass, one that made passing strangers stop and take a double take at the enchanted forest. All the trees were present, except for one. In the bottom right corner of the gallery, a paper that would complete the 3x5 square was absent. I stared deeply and scrutinized the empty bulletin space. I guess my cherry blossom tree would never deserve to see the world.

Growing up as an ABC, my American-born Chinese identity influenced many facets of my life. To be a Chinese girl, living in the Midwest, the epitome of American culture, meant my identity was in a constant tug-of-war between assimilation and self-expression. In the third grade of elementary school, for Valentine's Day,

I brought Chinese white rabbit candies to share with my class. My classmates disliked the rice paper that enclosed the candy and discreetly spat them out into the trashcan. So, from that year on, I brought Sweethearts candy hearts and Hershey's Cookies 'n Creme bars instead. To this day, I still have to remind my mother to not put traditional Chinese guava candy, 宏原番石榴夹心糖, or leftover pineapple cakes, 鳳梨酥, into the candy basket out of fear of driving away the trick-or-treaters. In many ways, I cut off the "branches" from the tree of potential in my life by subtly denying my heritage and culture. During the summer of freshman high school, I permed my hair out of hatred for my old, pin-straight hair. I spent so much of my time outside, neglecting wearing sunscreen for so many years that I tanned quite harshly. My skin turned to a darker shade, the polar opposite of the white, fair skin in Chinese beauty standards. My mother would always call me 焦糖, or burnt caramel. Likewise, contrary to my father's distinct palate for all kinds of seafood dishes (fishballs, garlic scallops, egg foo yong, salt-and-pepper squid, Cantonese salted fish, etc.) I despised seafood. The dish I despised most was 紫菜湯, seaweed soup. I hated the way the seaweed tangled in the back of my throat, threatening to strangle me. I hated the dark murky colors of the soup that obscured whatever poisonous spices hid within. I hated the bitter aftertaste that stayed on my tongue for hours. My family always teased me, calling me "Nebraskan girl" due to my refined taste buds' liking to only a handful of select dishes. Not to mention, growing up in a conservative middle school also exposed me to many racial microaggressions that caused me to want nothing but to dissociate from the only thing these other kids saw: my skin color. My favorite insults included the distasteful jokes about dog-flavored foods during lunch, the "bat-eater" comments throughout the COVID-19 pandemic, and the non-ceasing "ling-ling" nickname that haunted me like a "kick me" sign taped to my back.

However, this wasn't to say that my tree was completely dead. In many ways, I still thrived in my label as a Chinese girl. There wasn't a moment when my brothers and I would miss going to the local Asian Market grocery store. There, we lingered in the candy aisle for hours, choosing which amusing animal-shaped container we wanted with our lychee jelly, drooling at shrimp chips, and giggling over the off-brand Cheetos and Doritos. We could spend hours looking at the crabs and fish in prison-like confined aquariums and tapping the glass to watch the creatures dance. We loved to play hide-and-seek inside the mountains of rice bags. I still took Mandarin lessons to the highest class, AP Chinese. I loved the Autumn Festival, where my family would sit in idleness on the porch. In those memories, we only enjoyed each other's presence while nibbling our moon cakes (月饼) and sipping green tea. Chinese Lunar New Year also held a special place in my heart, as my church bonded together by folding 饺子, dumplings, and singing traditional songs to welcome the new year. Each year I saved my lucky red sweater just for this occasion. Additionally, I began to accept my label as I surrounded myself with peers similar to me in school, extracurriculars, and my church. It brought me ease to know that someone had grown up with the same childhood as me, someone had the same features as me, someone had endured the same fears and insults as me, and someone understood every thought that could ever cross my mind. Seeing how they accepted themselves unconditionally and expressed themselves, regardless of their skin color, replanted a cherry blossom seed in my heart.

Years down the line, just like in that Mandarin classroom, I continued to struggle walking into rooms. I noticed that I seemed to linger in the shadows of my beloved friends. While I developed interests that were similar to them, interests that were stereotypical to all Chinese children, I always stood in the shadows and never in the limelight. I could play violin well, but never well enough to join the all-state orchestra like them. I could play tennis well enough to make the school's junior varsity team, but never well enough to make varsity to compete with them. I could join my school's IB program and obtain good grades, and still never be as intelligent in standardized testing as them. I could have friends, but never be as much of a naturally extroverted social butterfly as them. Although my tree began to grow, it was only just a weak sapling, while their sakura trees dominated the sky, absorbing all the beams of sunlight and tourists' pictures. This hurricane of envy that was fostered yet suppressed was a constant reminder for me that still, in any room I walked into, I could be a participant, yet never a winner. In a courtyard full of accomplished gardeners, I couldn't even plant a seed. In a classroom of gifted artists, I could merely doodle. The color of my skin, and my identity as a Chinese girl, could provide me with a supportive community and a vivid culture to learn from. Yet the duality of it also leaves a permanent stain in my memory that I am held to a high standard in whatever I do.

I still find myself sitting in that classroom, surrounded by people I belonged with yet at the same time could not compare to. However, despite the mental breakdowns over identity crises at 1 AM and the imposter syndrome thoughts, this time, I do not run out of the room. I do not isolate myself in a bathroom stall. Instead, I seize a tissue from the Kleenex box in the far corner to blow my nose, return to my seat, and grab a new sheet of white paper. A clean slate for endless possibilities, independent from my history, my flaws, and my previous attempts. Because although my progress and achievements may not compare in magnitude to others, my progress itself is living proof that perseverance prevails. My success is not compared to those of others, but rather to myself. This time, my tree will blossom, engulfed with breathtaking sakura flowers. This time, my tree will have a strong foundation of a trunk to keep me rooted in the ground. This time, my branches and twigs may be lopsided and asymmetric, even sinking my tree, but my cherry blossom will stand. This time, my cherry blossom tree will make it into the glass gallery.

Bullfish

Lilly Pfeilsticker

Grade 12. Ft Calhoun Junior Senior High School, Fort Calhoun, NE. Sara Gross, Educator.

Fragrant purple irises lined the border between my grandma's driveway and the neighbor's lawn. The summer air was just warm and humid enough to irritate, and we were sitting on the beige leather seats of my grandma's car. She got into the driver's seat and turned the key. My wired off-brand earbuds were playing too loud. They were connected to my aunt's hand-me-down iPod and armed with music my mom downloaded a decade ago and what my preteen self had within the last year. Beyond this eclectic mix, I could hear the never-ending flow of must-be-nonsense from my towheaded brother, Sam, beside me. The harmless jibber-jabbering and periodic pokes from the kindergartener were enough to make my skin crawl and run me up the wall. Before long I snapped and hit my brother. Much to my frustration, he did not seem to learn the lesson I was teaching with "shut up"s and fists. Although, after a while I was yelling and sending a swift hand his way for anything.

"Lilly, stop that!" My grandma turned back from the front seat with exasperation building in her voice. "You're such a bullhead!"

The specifics of what a bullhead was escaped me, but I felt the sting. I furrowed my eyebrows and shot my grandma a defiant face.

"What's a bullhead?"

My grandmother had been essentially retired my entire life on account of an accident where she broke both her wrists. Despite not returning to formal work, Grandma refused to give up fishing. This must have been on her mind when she had scolded me.

"A mean fish."

Honestly, I thought it was just her way of calling me a bully.

My brother, now in middle school, and I, a year away from graduation, were on the sandy shore of the lake—more so an exaggerated pond—we have had our camper near for years. Sam had been fishing all weekend from dusk til dawn and sometimes beyond that. He would only pop back up at the camper to fix his poles and to take a *Simpsons* episode-length break from the sun. He had been asking me to come fishing with him, but I declined due to the temperature. The summer sun had gone beyond being slightly irritating to being in the misery-inducing range of the 90s that weekend. Respecting my boundaries had never been a strength of his, but in the past few years, Sam had grown more and more respectful. He understood and let me be.

Now, though, it was around 5 PM and the temperature had decreased significantly. I had been in my dry swimsuit all day wanting to swim, but no one would come with me. I approached Sam about a sort of compromise where we would fish together for a while, and then swim. It was a deal. We drove down onto the beach and he began fiddling with the poles and lines.

We never really got to the swimming because as I waited for him to set up our poles I was struck with a brilliant idea. I sat in the shallows. Little sunfish and bluegill weaved lazily between my legs and the sandy floor. Sure, if I moved to touch them they would escape me easily, but usually the tip of one of my fingers would be able to make contact with the fish's thin tail fin.

"Sam, we'd probably have more luck if we made a hand-sized pole with just some line, a hook, a worm, and a stick," I called back to him.

Looking up from his pole and scanning the beach, he responded, "Maybe, but we don't have any sticks."

"Pshh, there are sticks all over the place! We're in nature."

"Well, unfortunately"—I loved that for a twelve-year boy he had such diction sometimes—"we also only have one hook."

I trod out of the water and onto the shore. "I can find a stick pretty easily. Then, I guess we can go back to the camper and grab another hook."

Just then, it was like a lightbulb appeared over his head. "Earlier I saw a hook stuck in the fountain!"

So, I went to the edge of the beach and searched for small sticks; he attempted to unstick a hook from the floating fountain. I returned with the sticks quickly, but Sam was having less luck. The fountain was a small and decaying wooden platform with a flag and some plastic pipes pumping lake water out. It was held afloat by a hollow plastic barrel fastened to it. My brother clung rather pitifully to the side, desperately clutching one of his pricy fishing tools in his free hand.

"Lilly," he said while struggling to keep his grip on the clippers and the fountain, "can you come hold this?"

I swam out to him and after a pathetic amount of time and an impressive amount of teamwork, we pried what turned out to be the smallest ever hook out of the wooden platform. We hurried back over to his poles. Sam skillfully cut his line off his pole and put the worms on the hooks.

"Thank you, Sammy," I said, wrinkling my nose as I watched him skewer the dead worms for me. He answered by telling me he was just glad I came to spend time with him. I told him I was glad too. We wrapped our respective lines around our sticks and held the middle of our sticks.

Sat in the sand shallows again, he huddled over my shoulder as I gave it a try. There were lots of little bites with no real luck. Eventually, a rather large sunfish didn't look carefully enough. I yanked it up out of the water. The evening rays of sun shone through the water and glimmered off the dripping fish in an exquisite cinematic shot. Only for it to promptly drop off the hook and plop back in the water. We could not be bothered by the fish's grand escape. In that moment, we became convinced that we were possibly the coolest people on Earth. My brother and I beamed together and exchanged excited "did you see that?!"s.

We saw many fish that night. Sam informed me some were small-mouth bass. Others were bluegill. Quite a few were sunfish. I spotted some that appeared to be some sort of hybrid. But most importantly, there wasn't a single bullhead in sight.

SENIOR PORTFOLIO

Through High School

Ana Brock

Grade 12. Boys Town High School, Boystown, NE.

Sleep

Sleep
I may think I am ready to give up
But am I?
I lie in bed all night and day waiting for my mind to get in the right lane
The creeps and pains inside my brain
They're the ones that are keeping me awake
I try to push them away
All I need to do is lie and sleep
I say I can't keep doing this
I have to stay safe
I need to stay here
I have to keep myself awake
My dreams can't haunt me
My life is here
My arms are witness to the pains I feel
I am here
My mind's chains have locked me down
I have to sit here and cry and pray
Hopefully my life will all be normal some day
I am strong
I am here

I will no longer let these things haunt my brain
Trying to tear my future away

His Shelter

Life blows hard and knocks her over
The words hit hard and take control of her
The beatings hurt hard and leave a physical mark

He comes over like a guard to protect her
His kiss never forgotten
His smile revealed his soul
His eyes are just like the summer's sun
His personality forever more can be
He stands over her as she shall never be damaged again

Earth Is Me

I am the Earth
I am the ground that holds the feet of everyone around me
Without me they would fall without anywhere to go
I am a guide
Making way through the messy woods that we call life
I am the rock
Crushing everything that tries to break down my family and friends
I am the spy
Knowing your hurt and trying to help in any way shape or form to make you better
I am the provider
Giving the clothing off my back before you go a day without
I am the teacher

Trying to inform you of any harm coming to you even if you don't want to hear it
In reality I am still me
I am stubborn
Not liking change and not accepting it
I am soft
Crying at night and hoping others' pain will go away
I am scared
Of what is coming tomorrow towards my way
I am lost
Feeling like I am not good enough
I am messy
Tripping over my own feet
I am confused
Hoping people see the things that I do for them one day
But this is me and I am the Earth that surrounds and protects everyone else from the sun's harmful rays

My Mind's Chains

I lie down at night
Thinking this will all be over some day
I have to keep wondering all night and day
All my mind wants to do is run and play
I am trying to tell my mind to
STAY!
STAY!
STAY!
Honestly why?
I am no longer safe in my thoughts
My mind's chains have locked me down
I try to pry away the pain
I am no longer safe in the chains of my thought

I am no longer safe at all
Can I break free?
Can I let go?
I could forgive, but my mind says hello
No longer am I trying to break free
I have too much to do
I have too much to say
I can go nowhere but here
My mind's chains hit the wall saying
BANG!
BANG!
BANG!
BANG!
Everyone else around me just hears
I'm, okay?!
I'm, OKAY?!
    I'M, OKAY?!

Do U Even Care?

Did you know how much you left to bare?
Were you aware?
Did you even care? Did you even care about my health or wellbeing?
The few birthdays you showed up guaranteeing that a new man was
    in your front seat.
I aint blind, I can see the dumb things you're doing instead of
    seeing me.
There is a key to my heart that you have never seen because the
    drugs are holding you instead of you holding me.
So much I have been through could've been changed if you were
    there to see me grow and play.
Instead you were lying there on your bed like a bum with me grow-
    ing every day without even coming to say hey.

But I am not worried because look at what I have become without you.
I have grown and changed, but you can too if you dig yourself out of your grave of unchanged ways.
I hope to achieve great things in the future, but you have to be willing to be able to change for not just me or anyone else but be willing to change for yourself as I have changed for myself.
Honestly it's hard to say how you have been doing because it's hard to know if you have OD'd on the drugs you are taking or in hospital because of the poor choices you're making.
But you know, like I said, I can't change you for me, only you can change you for you, just know that I care about your wellbeing and hope you're okay.
They say that good things take time, but have you put in the effort for the good times to change you?

The American Dream, Right?

They promised the American dream, I see an American Nightmare
I see the black man always getting accused because of the color of his skin
I see the Natives not being able to be themselves
I see the Muslims not being able to pray in school because it's forcing religion on others
I see the Latinx community always getting asked if they have papers, even though they're fourth generation Americans
I see the people in the LGBTQ+ community getting fired because it's not socially acceptable
But this is the American Dream, right?
The black man is arrested
The white man walks free
The black man is murdered
The white man is released

But this is the American Dream, right?
I see the homeless, dreaded and abused
I see no home to go to or bed to sleep in or use
But this is the American Dream, right?
I see the children without any food
I see the tents lined along the shoot
I see the mom working and still not making it far
I see the family sitting in a trailer hoping they'll be okay
But, this is the American Dream, right?
I see you trying
I see you moving
I see you pushing

...

To see that America is not a dream, it's a nightmare

...

...

That we need to wake from and see.

The Inner Scaffolding of a Seventeen-Year-Old

LILY THOMPSON

Grade 12. Southeast High School, Lincoln, NE.

Commedia

Make me believe in
a higher power. Give me
the Comfort of God

Who can hold and hate
me? Let me be wrong, let me
lie in a burning tomb

To my own degree
let me boil in blood for his
molded Perverse Son.

Let me become thorn
brush and cry knowing the scold
dead are above me

In righteousness like
lies with likeness. Pleasure in
knowing he receives

Pagan prayer, child
fists yearn in touch with his cause.
What circle will thou

Send my short soul now?
she-wolf, leopard, lion. Stake
Out my sin against

His. Length sows no heart
rule bends him to man and beast.
When and to what degree?

We Made Breakfast Together Like Lovers Do

We laughed like soulmates do; we bickered like bats
in the night. You combed through my hair like lovers couldn't
    do right.
I struggled to sleep like home.
I woke with peace only
under your New York covers brought.
I ended my fall much before you. Morning meowed; I sought to
    rouse you and you were always
    resentful of it.
But the alarms did not make breakfast and your cats did not like
    me as much as I wanted.

You gave me gifts like I was sick—you loved so much I nearly
    thought it was a trick. I loved so much I didn't think of the days
    where you wouldn't find me.
Never did I think I would have bit you; hardly did I think I would
    like smoking so much.

There, there, then I wasn't. Then it wasn't—glowing warm, cherry
    and red
    my knees and temple begging
you
    with open palms

Outstretched, not to knight—not my apology.

Near to always I hated your mom; like assholes do
Wilted when you couldn't admit the burn.
I had your back like backstabbers might
not.

Together we're friends. Severed two or was it one
  two
over three and you were my one

Together we were girls, bunnies, boy and martyrs—we were friends.
  It wasn't something to explain away by
  Magnet hearts, Polaroids of the hours
hanging around my neck like budding rosary; pricked, dug deep
  into corkboard across my one bodied bed.

It wasn't something like anything else.
It was nothing to be worded right nor wove wrecked into
  my sorry so apologies.

We were friends.   We were
  friends and I am still sick.
We were friends and I still can't knit.   We were
  friends and my dog has died.
We were friends and there is no cat for me.   We were
  friends and the rabbit has passed.
We were friends and I don't expect to find you   (two
  rights, one left, second home)
on my steps   to ask
  me how death was.

Lapine the III: Gentleman Wolf

I had no clue: of course, fur under soft
skin, I swear to you, and neither did they.

I had not always felt: like the black sheep, in our story books
Maybe I did, maybe they knew.
Did you? See: the glint in mine eyes, star: white, shinier: even
than the unbrushed wool of an odd sheep.
I tried to be one—believed even

If only I pursued harder to scarf down dewy grass
The Hunger, blowing my pupils sable: body blanched, would not—
did not—exist.

It's instinct, a gut feeling
taught or not, sheep are bound to fear
The Slaughter: He hides behind barbed fences
tales over fire, tell of blood
not brought from birth.

Under their claws: the meat of my lamb
in between their teeth is the coat of me.

I've seen it, I swear to you
I was not taught; to be scared
of all wolves
Dress up in suit and tie, ask you to prom, take out your friends—
teach messy boys to wear white.

I didn't ask to be a nesting doll
I swear to you

Under their claws is the blood of me
in between teeth: the scraps of mum.

The Farmer created feed.
He left us
Mend the wine, shear my sheep!

I didn't ask: for labor
I *want* to be right
Yet, there's Gray: snagging from under my skin, dressing limbs in places that ought to be born sheer—naked.

There's a yellow to my teeth that soil stained grass did not bring.
There's a taste of iron to my tongue that sheep should not thirst for.

I don't even like wolves—I do not
Resemble: the ones that take sisters out to dance
Like: the ones that act as if the tie their Father clipped shows self-control.

Wolves Play;
Act 1: as if the cloak mother sewed is not sweating with blood, sitting dirty, in the cupboards behind holey garters.
Denouement: hunger

Everyone *gets* Hunger
But no one *starves* like a wolf.

You cast sheep's eyes at my ribs.
What big teeth—what bad breath!—You smell
that stench of spoiled blood taken

bled from the skin, blood not born of mother's needle and stitch or
Father's clip.

I've given up, not in the mood—being a sheep
lock her in a closet, let her out to play around other even
white coats.

She still has: a wolf's snout
Still smells: the stench of corse.

In the Stygian cage. Still and watch me grow skinny.
Maybe they always knew.
But now, *watch It:* dripping from fur, oozing out orifices like ink,
like blood, like tears, like sweat—*like stars*
the hunger in my throat is still here.

Stronger and I, am still scared.
I won't wear bow ties or show up with flowers for the daughter.

I try not: to bare my gums.
I will pierce my ear and shave my teeth
I will tell you of my self-restraint
I will give you the lead just in case.

Pictures

I don't take pictures unless I know the subject will be gone soon.

Funny thing is: everything will be gone (eventually)
Everyone knows this
Change happens. It never sits still; impossible to pose disappearing
once you've developed.

I photograph what's pretty mostly
I photograph because I have a bad memory
mostly, because I want to see how they were
mostly, because I know change will ghost onto sun-stained pictures
sometime
soon.

I photograph new places.
I pick trash because the flowers we smelled will wilt.
Because I can't bring back all our subway tickets
bottle caps, & the ice cream wrappers
of our favorite place
We won't ever be again.

I can't tape all pebbles to my notebook or pin all strangers to my
wall.
It's unbecoming: to grow mold from the orange we shared &
only I hung onto.

So, we take pictures
The old baby blue paint & peeling laminate tile of Home happen to
be there.
Just like the pleather couch with first pet's scratches
Just like cousin's old haircut & family's young faces.
In frame & out
they watch

You open presents of a birthday long gone.
There's the shirt you gave away, the gift
you were embarrassed to open but pleased to get.
Later: a candle will get blown out & you'll wish for
the same end as last year.

Later: cards with their periodic promises of love
will get thrown out &
you'll wish for the same change as last year.

We flip back
to pictures of that little daughter's first day of school
captured: a nervous, happier face.
Ah, there's the backpack you never grew into but got rid of when-
ever warranted.
Oh, here's that ugly haircut; bobbed, a little pony
straying to the side inside a tinnie tiny rubber band.

You & the dust still hold the stuffed animal you took
to school to help you along
Sister still remembers when Bunny was hers instead.

We flip back
to pictures of the dog, she's up to your armpit
sitting patient.
God, there's the polkadot pajama set you loved—you'd forgotten
about.

We take pictures because we want to remember before
their muzzles & paws turn gray & go cold.

We take pictures of Dog; getting bathed outside
because they look silly & we're having fun.
Their gray muzzle & her tired eyes just happen
to be there.

I'm tired of taking: pictures. I'm tired of collecting: trash being sad
that paper wrapper got ripped an' blew away.
Tired

having to get all the right moments
glued down
just so
I can miss more intimately later.

I wish parents hadn't taken photos of that child.
I wish I could ignore wrinkles on Adam & Eve's faces.
I wish I didn't hate that birthed form & flowering grin.

The funny thing is: change happens regardless
Yearning slithers, sliding up throat, candying soul.
You never come to fruition correctly, never ripen how you're supposed to, or taste as sweet as the first bite.

So, we wish.
I wish: photos were Grand Time Machines
I wish: the same thing as last year because I know they are not.

I dream: Oh, to feel Sun hugging her & Joy's juvenile smile peck atop her head
the beautiful small
the neverending nervousness of Little One
the firsts, of frivolous things.

I dream: to walk barefoot
on Home's carpet, in Adam & Eve's sanctum
once more—when I wasn't just a rotten core. When I had skin left to shed under the covers.

I pray: to light up in flames
shine stars across Sister's ceiling & feel like that was
our whole world

just me, as her, & Sister, in Home, giggling to Night as if Mom & Dad & Dog didn't hear
us loud & clear.

I beg: to return to the dirt of the apple tree
To release the grip around your ambered, candied throat.

I dread: the flash of the camera on my scaled skin.
I blow out the candle & try again.

Kit

My dog wears a t-shirt
(he's got the plague.)

My mother has gray hairs.
My dog must wear a t-shirt
he has boils and pustules and bundles of nerves bubbling from his skin
—he's got a gray maw and kind cloudy eyes and: he has the plague

The Black Plague
Killing: 10 + 6 million

My Grandpa has the plague too
he's got baby hairs: white and wispy
Grandpa chooses to wear a hat more now than before (Bahama divers, tan, red, white square)
Grandpa has to wear a t-shirt
(he has a hole to his heart under there)
his pants don't fit so well anymore.

The Black Plague.
Kills 10 + 6 million

My Grandad has the plague too
he's got to puncture more holes in his belts
Grandad has to wear a t-shirt too
(he has tubes to his gut under there)
he's got lots of room in his house, much more now than
before: Dec 19th, 2022

Nana gets to rest near a famous football player
60 + 3 minutes: away
Sealed behind
Limestone in a butterfly jar
Nana didn't have a lot of gray hair, she dyed it
(at her salon: I've never been)
she had lots of attributes
and plagues
Nurses said they hadn't seen someone like her (survive that long)
My mother says I look like her
My father says nothing; dreaming of sparrows and business.

Life kills
(7 billion + 900 million)

The plague kills
18,100,000 + 6,000,000 have to survive

Drugs and Brains and Disease kill too
unique: like t-shirts and hats and clothes and good-smelling
tobacco smoke
(The airport lost My clothes.)

Some of them got to be mine when Nana died but they're somewhere new now.
(kids suitcase, 13"W × 8.5"D × 21"H, Black)

I hope they come home soon
I hope I don't get grays
(or more plagues)

That's Life / I Love You / Don't You Read This

When did these ceilings become touchable?
When was it that I could no longer wrap my body around your leg and have you carry me whole? Now you carry a doll, shivering as I'm out onto the night.

When was it we met eye to eye, their wrinkled corners and aging hue?

You stopped pulling your hair out over me
now, I notice gray growing back.
Since when could I see up there?
I despise knowing: eye to eye.

Lift me up, for a closer look
Lug me around and pull me close
Pat me on the back and let me tear you apart.

Kill me with a kiss on the temple
Gut me with your sunflower song, preserve me in fluid and frost all your favorite parts
Won't you? Spread my blood across your lips
My gooey shine makes you look young again.

Live and stay alive, in the taste you birthed.
Take off your mitts and breathe me in.

You told me I'd always be your little one
just hold me close, I welcome you this time; mind wants, force laxes
the sinews.

Sing to me again
though I should be the Seraphim,
you'll take my tongue, and
I won't have to ask.
Tear my poison away: hair from gum
Cut the love away: gum from hair

www.ingramcontent.com/pod-product-compliance
Lightning Source LLC
Chambersburg PA
CBHW011225190726
48287CB00008B/2748